Education and the Death of Love

Also by Roy Stevens
AN APPROACH TO LITERATURE

ROY STEVENS

*Education and the
Death of Love*

LONDON
EPWORTH PRESS

7162 0292 1

Enquiries should be addressed to
The Methodist Publishing House
Wellington Road
Wimbledon
London SW19 8EU
Printed in Great Britain by
The Garden City Press Limited
Letchworth, Hertfordshire SG6 1JS

*For Jonathan and Penny
and their generation*

Acknowledgements

I should like to thank the Principal, governors and staff of the College of Ripon and York St John (or, to be accurate, of St John's College, York, as it was at that time) for making it possible for me to take leave for one term in order to complete this book.

I should also like to thank three typists who have laboured long at my not always easy and frequently-altered manuscript. Mary Mindenhall saw the book's early drafts take shape under her hands, and her meticulous work helped me greatly to see the way forward at this stage.

My wife, Judith, saw the book through its middle stages, and has given not only skilled secretarial help but also constant encouragement and advice to me. If the book has worthwhile insights, more than one or two are hers.

Catherine James typed the final draft of the book. Like Mary and Judith she was occupied with the cares of a household and family but like them she managed to work with exceptional care and insight. For her time, patience and efficiency I am very grateful.

Thanks also to Pam Ward for her valuable last-minute secretarial help.

I must pay a tribute also to the many members of staff and many students I have worked with. I have been privileged to know colleagues whose priorities, it has seemed to me, have been right—who have asserted with courage the supreme importance of people, often against many adverse pressures. Their warmth and friendship and humour have meant much to me. They have taught me a great deal, one or two especially, about the possibilities of a staff–student community. I am particularly grateful to my friend and former colleague, Terence Copley, at one time Senior Lecturer in Religious Education at my own college, now Director of the Sixth Form at Westwood High School, Leek. His insights and constructive criticisms have been of inestimable value in the making of this book, and his comments have been enriched by his own contribution to a caring college life.

I am equally grateful for those students, in college and at university, who have demonstrated by their openness, seriousness and readiness for dialogue, as well as by their warmth and laughter, that friendship and affection between staff and students may co-exist with academic order.

I am also grateful to the following for permission to reproduce copyright material:

Leila Berg, for permission to quote from *Neill Summerhill, A Man and his Work* a pictorial study by John Walmsley, published by Penguin Books; George Theiner for his translation of *School* by Miroslov Holub, from *Poetry of the Committed Individual* edited by Jon Silkin and published by Penguin Books; The Student Christian Movement Press Ltd for quotations from *Enough is Enough* by John Taylor, Bishop of Winchester; the *Sun* for material from Clare Good's review of *Savage Luxury* (25.9.70) and from Jon Akass' 'Let's all Run Over Cars for a Change' (27.9.72); *Woman* for material from 'Twice in a Lifetime' by Jane Anthony (10.5.75); Basil Blackwell and Mott Ltd for extracts from 'Assumptions Underlying the use of University Examinations' by A. N. Oppenheim, Marie Jahoda and R. L. James, published in *Universities Quarterly*, Vol. 21 No. 3. I am also grateful to the following for permission to reproduce copyright material: Mr Thomas H. Band for an extract from a letter to *The Times* of 1.7.69; the Bristol Medical Association for extracts from *So Now You Know about Smoking* by Dr Alfred Yarrow (Family Doctor Publications); the Cambridge University Press for publicity material for Professor Ian Lister's *Deschooling*; the *Guardian* for material from issues of 30.12.66 and 7.4.67; The Methodist Publishing House for an extract from *Unyoung, Uncoloured, Unpoor,* originally published by the Epworth Press; the General Secretary of the National Union of Railwaymen for quotations from the N.U.R. Golden Jubilee Souvenir of 1963; the *New Statesman* for extracts from its leader of 13.5.66; Dennis Burgess and the Editor of *She* for extracts from 'How do you define dirt?' in the issue of October 1971; Messrs Colin MacInnes, David Dungworth, Paul Thomas, Araminta Wordsworth and Eric E. Robinson for extracts from their articles in *The Times Educational Sup-*

plement of 2.5.75, 8.8.75; 25.4.75, 25.7.75 and from *The Times Higher Educational Supplement* of 25.7.75, respectively (© *The Times Educational Supplement / The Times Higher Education Supplement* London); the *Yorkshire Evening Post* for an item from their issue of 7.10.65; the *Yorkshire Evening Press* for an extract from an article by John Blunt, 9.6.66; for part of an article by Dr John Moorman reproduced by courtesy of the *Yorkshire Post,* 4.6.66. Mr John Wilson and Penguin Books Ltd for permission to quote from *Logic and Sexual Morality*; Mr Spike Milligan and Michael Joseph Ltd in association with M. and J. Hobbs, for 'New Members Welcome' from *Small Dreams of a Scorpion*; George Rawcliffe for his letter from the *Guardian*; the Hunstanton Town Council and the West Norfolk District Council for permission to quote from *Spree.*

I am also greatly indebted to Jonquil Hood, an indefatigable college secretary and good friend. Margaret Kidd helped with much preliminary typing while busy with many other commitments: I realize now how much this helped. I must also pay a tribute to my good friend and adviser, Roger Dixon, whose help at a crucial stage in the preparation of the manuscript was invaluable. Finally, very emphatically, I must thank the Methodist Publishing House: Rev. John Stacey for much-needed advice throughout; secretarial staff for coping with all my last-minute alterations and additions. I have been lucky in working with men and women whose efficiency has been all the better for a liberal helping of true Methodist warmth. To the General Manager of M.P.H., Albert Jakeway, I owe an enormous debt—for his ready help at all times, for his humour, encouragement and friendship.

Contents

Preface   13
Introduction—Wrong Models   17

PART ONE
Deceiving People   21
  1 Protecting Democracy   21
  2 Desensitizing (1) 'Earth and Air and Rain'   24
  3 Education for Violence—The Cult of Toughness   32
  4 The Fabric of Ordinary Life: A Time for Criticism—
    Three Sample Studies   40
  5 Criticizing the Social Fabric (2) Projects that Bite   55
  6 Peace and the People   63
  7 Bogus Social Discipline   71
  8 The Paradox We Do Not Face   76

PART TWO
Hurting People   83
  9 Getting People Worried (1)   83
 10 Getting People Worried (2)—Examinations   89
 11 Wasting People's Time: Desensitizing (2)   95
 12 Conclusions   99

PART THREE
Helping People   101
 13 Celebration   101
 14 Towards a New Life-style: More Freedom   105
 15 Towards a New Life-style: Creative Control   115
 16 The Supreme Task   123
 17 Planning   128
 18 Linking Up With the Churches   132
 19 Living With Half a Mind   138
 20 Proposals for Change   141
 21 Afterthoughts   152

Appendix A: Sample Research Material for Chapter 5   154
Appendix B: Sample Political Notes for Chapter 5   161
Select Bibliography   163

No one now denies that present-day education is beset with problems. The great expansion in schooling that has taken place over the past twenty years or so has given few of the results that were promised. Instead of a bright new age, we are confronted with vandalism, violence, truancy and a curriculum no one believes in. There are many schools, particularly in big cities, where no one willingly teaches and where it is very unlikely that much that anyone would admit to be education is being carried on. In many countries of the Third World the educational system is a wildly inappropriate importation.

From a notice of Ian Lister's Deschooling: A Reader,
(Cambridge University Press)

And we all have known
Good critics who have stamped out poet's hope,
Good statesmen who pulled ruin on the state,
Good patriots who for a theory risked a cause,
Good kings who disembowelled for a tax,
Good popes who brought all good to jeopardy,
Good Christians who sat still in easy chairs
And damned the general world for standing up.
Now may the good God pardon all good men!

ELIZABETH BARRETT BROWNING
Aurora Leigh, iv, 498–506

Preface

This book began life as a longish piece of writing addressed principally to teachers, lecturers and educational administrators. After working as a youth leader, as a schoolmaster, and finally as a teacher of teachers in a college and a university, I had become unhappy about so much being carried through and so much being planned for; I was also uncomfortably aware that the kind of unease I felt was not, on the whole, like the kind of unease being expressed currently by other restless people—those wishing to change one examination for another, Black Paper contributors, and the rest.

But—'Only connect'. The educational ferment of our time (perhaps 'ferment' is too creative a word—'chaos' might be better) is only too clearly related to political and economic troubles and to religious and moral crises of our age. First I found myself trying to reconcile the writing of a book on education with one on religion. True education, Alfred North Whitehead said, is ultimately religious—it 'inculcates duty and reverence'.[1] But then something else fell into place in my mind, a third, industrial-political, dimension; a vision of the kids tumbling out of school fresh from quadratic equations, and comprehension tests on *Northanger Abbey,* straight into the cities and on to the motorways and the sites for property developers, going home to silly adverts on T.V. 'Only connect'. The documentation for what is really going on is all over the place—not mainly in the educational journals, but in newspapers, magazines, news broadcasts; in advertisements and in the speeches of politicans. However, it is not fashionable for people in education to stick their noses into other people's territory (so defined), and if they do, they get into trouble.

This book attempts a non-party link-up between the

[1] Whitehead, A. N., *The Aims of Education and Other Essays*, Ernest Benn 1962, p. 23

separated areas of education, religion and politics, in homely, contemporary terms.

I stress 'non-party', in spite of a personal conviction that the work of successive governments in Britain during the 1960s and 70s, including all the issues those governments have neglected, has been disastrous for Britain and for Britain's children. I think it may have been as disastrous as the policies which spoilt Britain at the time of the Industrial Revolution.

I stress the link between education and politics because of what one might call the political failure of education, at home and abroad. We are rightly encouraged to remember the cruelties of nations and races whose ideologies were, or are, opposed to ours—Hitler's mass murders, communist slave-camps, and the rest. Yet it can still be a further source of concern to us that the most highly developed Western nation, with an enormous education budget, has recently fought one of the most disgusting wars ever conceived. In many Western nations there is increasing internal violence, as dissident groups, driven mad with dogmas, turn in resentment against each other. These are the vast and obvious issues, but inhumanity is deeply implanted in much routine social and political organization: for example, we have the statistically-minded and humanly unspeakable people who will not provide funds and resources for speed limit regulations and school-crossing patrols until a fixed number of children per mile have been knocked down—although money to the tune of millions can be found for road-making. The rottenness of a bureaucracy which sacrifices individual human lives, often young lives, to figures and to master-plans is inhumanity of a subtle kind, and it is spreading rapidly. It is spreading within the educational system. There are faculties of Humanities by the score, but what has happened to education in humanity?

I stress 'homely' because, having extended the subject-matter, I was aghast at the prospect of an enormous, semi-academic book for specialists, and so I have reduced it to a shorter book in simple terms on a simple plan for the general reader—for parents as well as teachers; for pupils too. This simplicity is not in any sense a form of condescension towards my own laziness or towards readers. If anything it is flattering. There are sufficient prolix and difficult books about education, and I think that some of us are unduly afraid of being

14

straightforward. I have a book of the learned kind on my desk now. It is about things like behaviouristic learning-theory, perceptive and cognitive development, latency, and the role of imitation. I have also a university M.Ed. syllabus before me. The remoteness from life of its academic terminology is remarkable—and frightening. There is a place for academic research in education, but I sometimes wonder whether work of this kind makes many people much happier. If such studies do point the way helpfully forward, we don't seem able to apply their findings adequately. So the present book uses fairly often the five-letter and four-letter words which find almost no place in education. I have noticed that they make the members of almost any public meeting on education, or any private committee, distinctly embarrassed—as if they had no place in the current vocabulary, as if someone had been sick on the carpet: I mean words like 'happy', 'peace' and 'love'. Love, happiness and peace, perhaps the most desirable of things, have been neglected, attacked and abused, it will be found, by the most unexpected agencies in education.

A final word—much of what follows is critical of some educational administrators, some politicians, advertisers, government agencies, industrialists, examiners; as well as some lecturers and teachers. I cannot emphasize too strongly that all that is said applies, in each case, obviously and inevitably, to some and not to all. In every area involved there are honest, scrupulous and compassionate men. It may be assumed that they constitute a majority. This reservation applies very specially to those who turn the wheels of industry. Nothing in this book is therefore intended to constitute an indiscriminate and total attack upon any one area. All the same, strange things have gone on, and are going on. I believe that hidden sub-areas of abuse, within many of these sectors, have had a substantial effect upon society. I also believe that these are radically and essentially the concern of education, if by education we mean in a practical sense the welfare of young people and of the world they inherit. The hurt done to people by some of these agencies is so great, that the best that can possibly be said is that many responsible men and women are the unknowing agents of policies of which they are not aware. And so my quotation from Elizabeth Barrett Browning must stand.

Introduction—Wrong Models

Most of us have been brought up half-consciously accepting a visual educational model. Most of us are dominated by two models, one half-consciously accepted, the other more or less unrecognized. Both are suspect, because both betray us.

The first is the model of the long, long path. Life is seen as a long and dangerous march through a wicked world, beset by snares for the righteous. The goal of eventual reward is always in the distance, always receding, but we go on sacrificing pleasure and love to it. In some sort of unspecified heaven, all that one has given up will be returned to one with a kind of compound interest, or so one gathers. This mode of thought is ascetic, almost monastic. I have a speech from a secondary school headmaster exemplifying this. He complains that his pupils do not give enough of their free time to his school, that they are tempted (*sic*) to attend too many evening activities, such as youth clubs, when they should be involved with homework. Most of the distractions (*sic*) can, he maintains, be delayed until after school years and examinations. Students must give everything up for the school and its work. Views like this are often sincerely held and made public in what are thought to be the best interests of pupils, who must 'get on'.

The virtues of effort and of the ability to give something up for the sake of something better are essential virtues, part of the truth about life. Unfortunately the model of the long trail to heaven brings with it serious temptations of its own. It over-emphasizes the ascetic aspect of life. It plays into the hands of people with more or less consciously cruel ambitions, who drive pupils hard for the sake of their own glory. It intensifies the dictatorial streak in any leader, who gradually assumes the right to impose not only work but also all his own standards on his pupils. It encourages aggression and competition; and it is worth noting that this moral or religious mode of thought—'Do this for the sake of your school, your God, your parents'—something which is very noble in the

17

beginning, shades somewhat ignominiously, in practice, into the worship of some very wordly things. The carrot in front of the donkey, the distant goal, sometimes even achieved, is often worldly respectability, the 'right' friends, a well-stocked drinks bar in an opulent home, the right number of children (a bit short perhaps on parental love); and prosperity may well have been gained by dubious commercial ploys. These are the rewards of the blasphemy of denying the present, and of the endless chasing of people, never letting them be.

Of course, the future we sacrifice our pupils and our own charity to is not the real future, the one we should be thinking about: the preservation and enrichment of future life and of the Earth itself. The model of the long, long trail a-winding sacrifices the present, but does not redeem itself with care for the future. It is really concerned with one thing—self.

The other model is more dangerous because it is largely concealed. This is the closed machine which we serve as we go through each day. In a pamphlet about school examinations published by the National Association for the Teaching of English, it is remarked that 'We are all caught in a machine'.[1] A student who tore up his exam paper at the start of an examination and walked out, said that his action had been a gesture of protest against a machine. 'People, not personnel'—'This university butchers brains'—such are the scrawlings on university walls. Some student gestures like these are purely irresponsible, mere covers for laziness, but not all. A university professor known to me, kind and humane, substantially helping to roll round a large department in which students often found themselves bewildered and made cynical, told me that he could not see a machine, that it did not exist. Uncreative processes breed their own blindness to lack of creativity.

While the long, long trail at least may have resting-places, the closed machine, the manic circle or spiral, offers little respite to us. Indeed the whole point is that people are so harried and hurried that they have no time to reflect on those things they are doing, and are not meant to. Teachers and lecturers who really want to teach, who want to be personal, in the best sense, complain more and more that they feel like minor civil servants snowed under with forms and statistics.

[1] N.A.T.E., *English Examined, A survey of 'O' Level Papers*, p. 44

18

They are caught up in a machine. Students caught in the same circular process, repeating itself monotonously each day, each term, have no time to reflect on the human implications of their subject. Examinations alone do not account for the machine, though it is worth remembering how recent is the mushrooming growth of examinations in this country (we treat them as if they were timeless). The mainspring of the machine is the growth of educational bureaucracy, producing endless bits of paper and endless meetings. The meetings weigh staff down with trivial detail, and while we are getting small points of detail right our main direction is wrong.

We can turn away from these two bad models and look at the one model which is right, the model of the family. In a good family, whatever its overall design, people come first. Joy, as Wordsworth said, is its own security, and love an unerring light. The present, not the exhausted day off or the silly booze-up after a debilitating round of committees, is the point. If we could cut down the forms, and send home most of the examiners, we might be able to fashion a school and college life which was like the life of an extended family, something not claustrophobic and tight and womb-like, but something caring and responsible and free. Such revolution requires money—money diverted from the building of missiles and motorways, and here we see the dreadful link-up between the military-industrial world and education: because the rockets and the roads are taking the money from education, money needed for a generous staff : student ratio, more choices of study, better senior secretarial help to relieve the administrative burden of teachers and lecturers; many more options; schools which are more cheerful and better furnished; and lots of equipment.

And if the remarks above are dismissed as sentimental, as they are sure to be by some, it could be argued that if you keep education as a mechanical, unfriendly thing much longer, you will get your vandalism and you will get your windows broken by young people who in their cynicism know that they are being betrayed. You may get your world blown up too, because nobody has been taught to care for it.

One must destroy the spirit of money, the blind spirit of possession. It is the dragon for your St George.

D. H. LAWRENCE
Letter to Lady Cynthia Asquith

Christianity is Art and not Money. Money is its Curse.

WILLIAM BLAKE
from the *Laocoön Plate*

PART ONE

Deceiving People

CHAPTER 1

Protecting Democracy

Parts 2 and 3 of this book deal with the obvious hurtfulness of much contemporary education and with the good it could do, and sometimes does. To clear the ground first, Part 1 deals with education's large and gloomy gaps, its deceptive omissions; and initially with its failure to encourage true democracy.

In all that follows I am concerned about democracy. Hundreds of thousands of people, men, women and children, have died for freedom. We pride ourselves on our 'freedom' and to some extent with reason, that we are not as other men are, at the mercy of the secret police, not mass-produced in one obedient pattern, as in some communist countries (and in some violent, anti-communist countries also). But are we so much better? We have no secret police as yet, but we have snoopers. Already Western industry is beginning to demand computerized personality tests of its personnel, involving huge invasions of privacy. Secret files are kept on many ordinary citizens, students especially; the police already know too much about us; we are 'different' at our peril, even if we are law-abiding. And if we protest publicly and peacefully on the streets about anything, we are usually photographed. The modern set-up, of cars for all, tobacco, endless drinking, the restless acquiring of gadgets; fussy, expensive entertaining and meals 'out', and high-speed living; has been fashioned for us. Alternatives have been blocked off, and this pattern of living is hammered home through all the media, even in the most innocent-looking films and shows. And all this goes with a great deal of social and sexual stereotyping, which is what industry wants: as in the vision of many futurist writers, we may finish as reliable robots geared to a meaningless

21

normality. Is our democracy really working? Have we betrayed those martyrs of old? And what has education to say?

We have fought appalling wars, and risk others yet more appalling, for the sake of 'freedom'. But how free are we? Are we trained to criticize the posters, the silly advertisements in the cinema, the slanted programme on T.V., the hate campaign directed against the Left (or the Right) laid on by politicians or newspapers? (Two of our extreme Right-wing papers and one of our party leaders have recently inaugurated an over-done and dangerously war-like hate campaign against the Russians. We are not trained, as a nation, to recognize slanted language or the dangerous half-truth.)

Have we really discovered how to make our mark democratically? And whose fault is it if protests are disregarded, even if we can still protest without being arrested? A good deal of the media is biased against students, and not only because some students are irresponsible: because students have not yet the glazed eyes of older people—they are still critical enough to criticize, to see. It is younger people who see both the need for protest and the present pointlessness of so much of it. A student wrote, while one of our Labour cabinets was in power—and the Left has traditionally been held to be sympathetic towards young people—'I am tired of criticisms of students who attend protest demonstrations. They protest because appalling injustices are committed, with the full backing of the authorities. "Why don't you write to your M.P.s?" people say. We do. We also send petitions to Mr Wilson and others. The trouble is, the constitutional channels for reforms are blocked by bureaucrats. If you put enough pressure on them they might consider putting your point of view to a sub-sub-committee. It is then rejected, filed and forgotten.'[1] How can we save the true democratic heritage, and who will save it if we in schools and colleges do not bother about helping people to care?

This book is not about violent revolution: it is about a way of avoiding revolution and avoiding war by making democracy work. Civilized democracy is the best safeguard against revolution, and democracy is withering because we are not trained to watch over it and guard it. A BBC programme, *This Island Now*, made reference to the swollen power of the

[1] *Sun*, 1.12.69

Executive, of events manipulated to ensure that nothing interferes with that power, of the power of lobbies to persuade Ministers to do just what lobbies want, of public protest which is too slow and too late. In another broadcast, for schools, a former party leader, who might reasonably be assumed to be well-informed, spoke of pressure groups and vested interests secretly acting 'free of any democratic process'.

To avoid revolution we need a democracy that works. We need responsibility, and ultimately we need people who love and care for the world. Just now education is meeting neither of these needs: we do not train people to use the instruments of democracy, and we turn them out with desiccated emotions so that they pursue power, not love; so that they do not see the wonder of the flower, the landscape to be preserved, the returning spring, the mystery of the heavens on a clear night. We need minds sharp and critical, but critical because they are enthusiastic and caring. Education is inadequately concerned with love, care and responsibility. We have made each other so hard-headed and afraid of caring that these things are considered effeminate and sentimental. And as most people know, enthusiasm is a major casualty of the educational rat-race.

It must be added that some of the material, presented as educational material, in the section which follows, is not conventionally educational at all. In some areas the writer on education will get into trouble for his sins of trespass, especially from those people who sincerely believe that democracy is working and that we have sufficient numbers of appropriately-educated people at the top running things for us. This of course is nonsense, as I hope to show, if only by virtue of the actions, or failures to act, of some of these people. Only educational guerrilla warfare across the frontiers between 'education', formally considered, and the world beyond it, is now enough.

CHAPTER 2

Desensitizing (1) 'Earth and Air and Rain'

The 'long, long trail' model ignores the present and takes a long time to 'reach' the future, by which time 'successful' people are inclined to be too exhausted to do anything except earn money and withdraw behind the white suburban fences. The circular model, with its endless vortex, allows little time for thought about anything except about getting through the day and returning forms to the person who is pestering one for them. Therefore the present, the precious present, is neglected; and so is the future. It is scarcely surprising that we use our Earth as if it were a gigantic ash-heap. We have no time for it.

Every gallon of petrol contains 2.7 grammes of lead, enough to provide a tolerable daily intake for 10,000 children; 11,000 tons of it come from cars in Britain each year. American research suggests that low levels of the poison cause changes in the behaviour patterns of children.

Two thousand children worked for the Advisory Centre for Education producing evidence to show that only in six areas of Britain was it still possible to breathe pure air. The Lake District Fells, Exmoor, most of the Scottish Highlands and Wales, and Hadrian's Wall, were found to be the only pollution-free areas. They handed this information to Mr Geoffrey Rippon, the then Environment Secretary. The Consumers' Association has pressed for teams of government inspectors to check Britain's tap-water, some of which has been found to be bacteriologically below World Health Organization's standards. Meanwhile, asbestos from car brake-linings is fouling air. Asbestos lung cancer has been foreseen as a disease likely to rival cancer caused by tobacco. Cadmium and mercury are also accumulating at or near dangerous levels as industrial by-products. Our food contains dangerous additives, colouring, flavourings, preservatives, the effects of which are not by any means fully known—the compulsory labelling of foods with a list of ingredients has

24

proved farcical, since it is rare to find any manufacturer actually giving the name of the stabilizer, colour, etc.

There is deep concern about the possible pollution of the sea on a catastrophic scale by virtue of the gigantic oil-tankers now in use; and concern too about the transport of dangerous chemicals by road. As a newspaper serving a large industrial area pointed out, the best way to transport dangerous materials is by rail, 'but the short-sighted closure of rail sidings and branch lines enables companies to take the easy way out of expanding their road tanker fleets.'[1]

Not least as the result of young people's enthusiasm, some cleaning-up has been accomplished, including the clearing of rivers and streams by student volunteers and the application of a wise and watchful science upon some major waterways. Other rivers, in which children once played safely, are now in many cases a disgrace. The Norfolk Broads are slowly 'dying', probably as a result of 'fertilizers'. In Yorkshire, the Ouse from Selby to the Humber is rated Class 3 on a pollution chart (poor), the Don Class 3 to 4 (poor to grossly polluted), the Dearne Class 3 or 4 for about a third of its length, the Rother Class 4 for almost its entire length, and the Aire Class 4 for most of its length below Bradford. Nitrates poured indiscriminately on to fields are proving, when they get into drinking water, a health hazard to young babies. It must be emphasized that this great second round of the pollution of Britain is environmentally far worse than the first round at the time of the Industrial Revolution. Even though sometimes visually less damaging, it is far more dangerous because of the advance in science, particularly of chemistry. Meanwhile there is concern about the effect of pollution on weather. Conservative M.P. Mr Philip Goodhart has asked the Department of Education and Science to initiate research into the weather. 'We are on the edge', he said, 'of an era in which the amount of pollution rising into the atmosphere will affect the weather.' In the United States not so long ago military men proposed the shooting of millions of fine needles into space, a procedure which might have effectively darkened the sky. A current concern as I write is about possible damage caused by freezer gases, from aerosols, to the ozone layer which filters through vitamin D and protects us from the

[1] *Northern Echo*, 9.7.73

sun's dangerous ultra-violet light.[2] Everyone knows about radio-active fallout from nuclear weapons' tests, and of course the catastrophic pollution after a nuclear war will probably mean the end of human life on this planet and of the life of warm-blooded animals, though ironically probably not of plants. At the level of ordinary life here and now there is already the growing litter of industrial rubbish, particularly of plastic throw-away containers. The failure of glass and paper re-cycling and lack of government interest in it is one of the unexplained mysteries of our time, and we are gradually fouling the Earth up with materials which could be re-used if we bothered enough. All this, as every environmentalist knows, is nothing like the whole story of what is going on, but the one major characteristic of the environmental issue is the way in which authority drags its feet so that preventative action is taken too late if at all. It is ominously true that this consideration applies to the prevention of nuclear war.

Only the language of sin and morality can match this total world situation. 'Debauching the Earth', writes John Vaizey of one industrial threat, and he writes of:

> . . . those forces in the modern world which drive the modern world into patterns of consumption that use ever more resources like copper, iron, oil and coal: for its own profit, it is part of a system that creates 'wants' and, to satisfy the creative wants, strips the Earth of its resources—leading to pollution. . . .[3]

And the Duke of Edinburgh has spoken of technology producing wealth while at the same time destroying places where life and leisure can be enjoyed.

> The present free-for-all system is thoroughly destructive. The general attitude to the oceans is reflected in their use as a gigantic rubbish tip.[4]

[2] Aerosols are now (1977) to be phased out in the U.S.A., but not in Britain, where a lot of money and work is invested in their manufacture. One's faith in British politics in relation to concern for the long-term protection of people and of the environment is again shaken. Short-term economic considerations alone seem to count. Surely here is a fertile area for Christian action: the global concern of Christians for what they feel to be God's threatened creation should be urgent and practical

[3] John Vaizey, 'Debauching the Earth', *The Listener*, 19.10.72, p. 509

[4] Melchett Lecture, 23.5.67

Vaizey is right in applying the language of sexual excess to this non-sexual area.

What do we do in education? We are too busy 'doing' set-books, novels, nouns and verbs, light and heat (unrelated to current problems), medieval drainage. 'Due to lack of interest tomorrow has been cancelled.'

If our children deserve a tolerable future they deserve to be given the weapons with which to fight for it. This means that an Environmental Studies syllabus should not end merely with 40 per cent for course work and 60 per cent for a three-hour paper. Pupils need to be made urgently, critically, positively and democratically rebellious, which is quite different from making them pointlessly vandalistic. To question! To question! Why does the Department of the Environment not act on lead additives in petrol? Why is there always so much damage done before checks and safeguards are put into operation? Why is it that, as Dr M. J. Chadwick, York University biologist, maintains, 'In many cases, government science on environmental matters seems unnecessarily remote and secretive'?[5] Under the present administration the Department of the Environment has shown occasional responsibility in defending the environment. At other times the oddest things have gone on; and it has seemed that the chief enthusiasm of this area of government has been to encourage the building of massive roads, one of the worst threats to the environment both for man and for animal life. In British Lakeland the much-debated link road through glorious countryside from A6 to the coast was authorized by the then Department of the Environment, securing the certain destruction of many beautiful features of the area—for example, the incomparable trees alongside Lake Bassenthwaite. The road follows in many respects the tracks of old railways, and the Department secured the closure of one of the two last surviving railways into Lakeland, along the line of the main road, at about the same time. Authority has been indifferent for years to the decline of public transport in this area, and Lakeland is handed over even more encouragingly to the car, although one can hardly conceive an area in which the car is more damaging. The Cambridge University Conservation Society has said that Britain is in danger of

[5] *Yorkshire Evening Press*, 19.2.73

sacrificing its national parks and beauty spots to a growing flood of recreational motorists. It calls for regular trains, park-and-ride facilities, and the abandoning of all motorways and major road improvements in national parks.[6] These sensible recommendations come from an environmental research group. Why do they not issue from the Department of the Environment itself?

Why was it necessary for another group of environmentalists to condemn a recent Secretary for the Environment as an anti-environmentalist, because he proposed to drive a motorway through the middle of an incomparable and historic country estate in order to save a diversion of two or three miles? Why did the then Secretary of State for the Environment overrule his own inspector in the case of the building of oil refineries on Canvey Island? In this case the inspectorate said that the loss of amenities to local residents outweighed the national interest. This one-time quiet residential island had already been saddled with the largest petro-chemical plant in Britain. Then the oil refineries were sanctioned. Comments from local residents, recently given publicity in a popular journal, make interesting reading:

'We couldn't believe it at first. . . . How could someone who hadn't even been to see the island make such a decision?'

'The smells nearly choke us . . . if we leave here, how do we get another house? . . .'

'And what about the elderly people? Some of them put every penny of their life savings into their homes, and now they are trapped.'

'. . . it seemed to us that the oil companies had made up their minds to come to Canvey—and to hell with the 30,000 of us who live here. If they got their way and built the oil refineries, we have six refineries within five miles of us.'

'We have more and bigger road tankers—our estimate is 842 of them every day, which means one every 102 seconds if they work day and night, or one every 34 seconds if they worked an eight-hour shift. . . .'

[6] *Yorkshire Evening Press, 19.2.73*

'. . . we women arrange our housework around the demos. We have been up to London I don't know how many times.'

'It is a pattern of life now. If we see a chance to protest, it's drop everything, and off. We've written, phoned, talked to important political figures and to the oil companies. It's like banging your head against a brick wall. No one seems to care that our lives are being spoilt.'

'There is a road on the island that some of the islanders call "the before and after road". On your right, as you drive along, there are still green fields, hedges, trees. A few ponies graze in the distance. On your left, a refinery is being built. The ground is scarred and torn. Trees and grass are gone. Giant machines move to and fro like robot dinosaurs. It is a nightmare landscape.'

'And they want to build another refinery on the right-hand side. . . . We found the remains of a badger one day. . . . They had ploughed a bulldozer right through its sett. It made us feel quite sick. And they set fire to a hedge, with the fledglings still in their nests. We begged them to wait—and they laughed.'[7]

In this case, one so obvious that any well-educated primary school child could judge of its merits in a moment, development has at last been halted and a further inquiry is to be held. The Herculean efforts of the local Member of Parliament have contributed markedly to this development. But many children leave school without any idea of the name of their M.P., or of how to contact him, or of his powers. They do not know what he can do for them—nor do they know of the limits of democracy, when, so often, members send back to their constituents polite letters from permanent officials 'higher up' simply saying that nothing can be done. Young people need education for survival—to know their killers. We do not do enough in schools to get young people to question the all-prevailing idea of industrial expansion at all costs. The life-blood of democracy is to question, question, question. What is really going on? Who is really being protected? What are the real priorities? How may we lobby peacefully, and demonstrate decently, without affront to the police or to public order? If this is not education, then we are educating robots who will simply get done to them what they deserve.

[7] Jane Anthony, 'Twice in a Lifetime?', *Woman*, 10.5.75, pp. 13–15

One longs for education which will encourage a seeing eye, and see not merely with love but also with a feeling for the whole of life. How right was Dr Norman Moore, of the Natural Environment Research Council at Monkswood, when he remarked, 'I sometimes think that the educational background of most politicians, which tends to be historical or legal, may be the main reason why they do not recognize the great problem of the day, which is essentially biological.'[8]

Here and there hopeful things are going on. A school in rural Warwickshire, as part of a summer-term project after the external examinations (*sic*), undertook a survey of public transport in its area, one in which there were no rail services, and no bus routes linking with the nearest railway stations.

> From the statistics collected it was possible to construct flowline maps to illustrate the travel pattern. . . . It was then possible to suggest improvements and extensions to existing transport. . . . A simple suggestion which came out of the survey was that all the bus companies should provide a complete timetable of services. A digest of the report listing the main recommendations was circulated to local councils and the press with requests for action. The project was popular with students and provided local groups campaigning for improvements in transport with accurate figures to back up their arguments.[9]

Congratulations to Paul Thomas and his pupils at Shipston-on-Stour High School for doing work which ought to have been done by paid government officials. This at least is real education. And it was 'popular with students'. But how rarely this sort of thing is done, and how little we do to make pupils see what needs to be done.

We do not even help them to see—*really to see*—what is happening in the cities. Says Colin MacInnes:

> . . . our educational system has consistently neglected the visual, aural, and physical faculties of the boys and girls consigned to its unworthy care. All the emphasis has been on learning words and numbers—on acquiring knowledge through the intellect, to the almost total neglect of the senses.

[8] John Whale, 'Pollution', *Sunday Times,* 20.12.70, p. 11
[9] Paul Thomas, 'Improving Public Transport', *The Times Educational Supplement,* 25.4.75, p. 33

Rising around us, we see buildings of incredible banality and crudity. Why do 'the public' accept such monstrosities so tamely? Must it not be because even a well-educated boy or girl can leave school, and even university, almost totally ignorant of the art of architecture? It is not that our children have no natural taste—their own paintings prove that they have it in abundance—but as they approach adolescence nobody helps to form their adult discrimination about good building. . . .

Further, if it is felt that science students should know something of the humanities (as well as vice versa), then teaching of the sensual arts to science pupils seems even more appropriate than that of partial literary studies.

He adds:

One can, of course, visualize the contempt with which this proposal would be greeted by those satisfied with an intellectually orientated curriculum.[10]

Is it too much to claim that education, because it does not give pupils these discriminating tools, is in effect an ally of a crude commercial system?

Support that some of us might look for from the churches is not forthcoming. 'Whom shall we send, and who will go for us?' The failure of religion to come to grips with this problem is a lamentable failure. 'Sin' is still sexual sin—that convenient bolt-hole. Few vicars, as they bless the farmers and the crops, think of the nerve-gas derivatives let loose on the soil, of the battery hens, and the calves standing motionless in semi-darkness through most of their brief, miserable lives; of the coloured plastic bags of artificial fertilizer which boost the crops for the moment and then impoverish the soil. The education system and the churches have failed to encourage that sacramental view of life, in its Monday-to-Saturday aspects, which is now not only contemporary religious truth but also urgent good sense. The Churches and the schools do not wish to be involved, to be real. They do not wish to see the devil leering at us all the time: cash, hard cash.

[10] Colin MacInnes, 'Bringing Them to Their Senses', *The Times Educational Supplement*, 2.5.75, p. 24

CHAPTER 3

Education for Violence—The Cult of Toughness

Enter a tree, bowing and saying:
          ˙ I am a tree.
A black tear drops from the sky and says:
          I am a bird.
Here now, approaching
          along a cobweb
              comes something like love,
                    and it says:
              I am silence.

But then there sprawls in front of the blackboard
          a national democratic
          horse in a waistcoat
          and repeats,
          pricking his ears to every side,
          repeats and repeats:
              I am the driving force of history
              and
              we all
              love
              progress
              and
              courage
              and
              the wrath of warriors.

And then from under the classroom door
trickles a thin stream
of blood.

For here begins
the quartering
of the innocent.

MIROSLAV HOLUB, 'School'[1]

The scene is a large maternity hospital serving a big British

---

[1] Translated by George Theiner, *Poetry of the Committed Individual,* ed. J. Silkin, Penguin 1973

city. Money is short in the National Health Service and staff are in short supply. Women in labour are told not to make a fuss, and are scolded, as if they were school-children, during the traumatic act of giving birth. Gas-and-air machines, which the mothers have been trained to use during excellent relaxation classes, are discovered not to be available. (The National Health Service is short of money because we have spent twenty million pounds on each Concorde and are busy changing the heads of our Polaris missiles.) When the child is born it is shown to the mother and father, and then put aside, so that the mother does not see the child for perhaps twelve hours. The immediate and vital love-bond between mother and child is prejudiced, and the mother may come to reject the child unconsciously to a greater or lesser degree correspondingly. Because the child is not immediately put to the breast the mother may decide against breast-feeding, and her uterus may not contract as it should because the child is not being suckled as nature intended. Breast-feeding will not be disparaged, but not encouraged much, either, and little help will be given to those interested. (No one has much time, and bottles are easier.) During the mother's stay in hospital the baby will be often rebuked if it cries and the mother will be repeatedly warned against spoiling it—'They can begin to get the better of you straight away—you have got to be hard and let it cry.'

Perhaps hospitals like these are now in a distinct minority. Thank God, many are vastly different. But, in some, negative attitudes prevail. A. S. Neill once remarked that men are made anti-life in their cradles. The scene described above is not that of a London workhouse in the 1880s, but of a British hospital in the 1970s. It is about care taken to reduce the love-bond, to reduce physical contact, to deny intuition, and to teach people to handle children as if they were parcels.

Results of similar training are evident not only in under-privileged families, in the normal sense of that term, and not perhaps principally in such families. Many children in prosperous suburbs with many material possessions are clearly not really loved, and suffer accordingly. They have been deprived at birth.

If a child attends a good primary school, and has played creatively with other young children in earlier years. his deprived emotional life may be compensated through involvement with other children and teachers. He may learn sympathy with others, the joy of language and of making things, sympathy with stars, animals, insects and flowers.

If he is one of a 'privileged' minority he may be sent at nine or even much earlier to a boarding school to teach him to be 'independent' and 'confident'. A move like this will give prestige to his parents. Unless the child has already been made insensitive, the move from home will result at first in much emotional distress, some of which will recur frequently until his feelings are calloused over. He must 'be a man and not blubber'. He will learn that it is shameful to want to be hugged and protected and cuddled, and soft to want to feel that you would like to be at home, and shameful to want to give and receive comfort by touching other people. He will do a great deal of competitive sport, some of it genuinely good fun, and some of it very violent. He will learn to cope with examinations, and gradually unlearn the love of cows and beetles and rabbits, for he must now attend lessons in which white mice are chloroformed and frogs dissected and cockroaches driven mad by being given electric shocks. But he will have to beware of sexuality and try to be 'pure', although he will be encouraged to enjoy films about war, death, stabbing, beating and shooting on cinema and T.V. screens.

The rest is predictable. We do not at the moment have compulsory military service in this country, but we are training people for war, toughness and competition, for fear and revenge. One wonders whether, unconsciously, the violence is, in fact, the pitiable act of revenge—for all the hurt.

I have used 'he' throughout: it is observable that many girls sent away, at the cost of much distress, to boarding schools, distance their own children from themselves in later life—sending them away in turn, even farming them out far too early to 'baby-minders' while they resume careers.

It is sad that the Church does so little to offset this. The military–industrial complex, about which even such a conservative as President Eisenhower warned us, demands a tough attitude. At school assemblies and degree ceremonies we sing of the King of Love who is our Shepherd, and ask for the help and guidance of God. In fact we are serving a machine equipped with all the things we are expected to accept without question—guns, missiles, rockets, fast cars, all the signs of death.

If anyone doubts the existence of the massive inconsistencies which mark our social life, it might be helpful to look at the mass media. Here the impact of television, and of our own reaction, or failure to react, to it, are paramount. For instance, at the end of 1974 and at Easter 1975 the country was regaled at the Christmas and Easter festivals of love and peace and hope, with, not one or two, but with a whole farrago, of violent films, on both television channels. A revolver looked out at us, deadly and rigid, from the Easter pages of one family programme-guide; the other portrayed 'The Battle of the Bulge' and a blazing American tank. Easter Day finished on one channel, immediately after another late-night parade of killings, stabbings and beatings, with the meditations of St Augustine! And the second Bank Holiday, formerly centred round the Whitsun festival of the coming of the Holy Spirit, was celebrated by the BBC in 1975 by a revival of *The Longest Day*, bringing back, along with so many films and film series put on by the BBC, the horrors and the *camaraderie* of war. Is someone trying to keep us ready for the killing?

Every night on television an American crime film ends with a punch-up: violence is to be regarded as normal. The ITV 'Summer Festival' of 1976 was featured by means of magazine covers in full colour showing warriors and thugs. In one case the cover, lying open to view on every bookstall, was made up of a composite picture illustrating, top left, an injured man falling to the ground with blood streaming down his back. Another man, revolver in hand, was apparently 'putting the boot in', while, below left, another smiling man aimed a double-barrelled gun out at the readers. The following issue carried a cover showing a man brandishing a dagger—another 'Festival' item. A film advertised as cinema family fare was publicized by a major film circuit by means of a poster illustrating, bottom left, torture, and top right, shooting: an enormous machine-gun occupied the centre, while below a ship was being blown up. (We could recall the sadistic pleasure shown by the audience watching war films during Hate Week in George Orwell's *Nineteen Eighty-Four*.) Yet if anyone dared to show on television or at the cinema

35

thoroughly candid acts of physical love, instead of measures which cause intense pain or death, tearing bodies and blowing people's organs to pieces, hundreds of folk connected with the Church or with education would shout 'Outrage!'. And this in spite of the pleasure inseparable from most forms of love, and the caring which it often goes along with, and its function as the giver of life which we all share. Yet there is hardly a squeak from the world of religion or education about the continuous mental bloodbath of violence and war. Why is it that we take coach-loads of adolescents out of school lessons to see films like *Waterloo* instead of (for example) films such as *The Virgin and The Gypsy*, the kind of story which is about reverence for life and for the senses—though it is pretty sure to carry an 'X' or 'AA' certificate! Why do our film censors appear to prefer riddled corpses and burning towns to healthy, joyous sexuality? Why is it that the only significant moral crusades against the media, sincere though they may be, confuse violence with love? Why is it that education is not encouraged to do anything about refining public taste?

One wonders when education will come out of its syllabus-bound hidey-hole at least to notice, and perhaps comment on, if not to act about, influences of staggering importance to it outside the classroom. Crucial here is the double standard affecting the portrayal of sexuality and the portrayal of violence. The film critic of the *Times Educational Supplement,* a lonely voice, excellently makes the point about sex. Complaining of the banning in England of a foreign film, *The Empire of the Senses*, because of its real (not simulated) portrayal of sexual love, he concludes, 'I feel that awareness of the acts of intercourse in the film marks an important step in the de-mystifying of sexuality that seems crucial to any progress towards health'; and he concludes that the act of censorship reveals our society as 'a thoroughly sick society, both repressive and repressed'.[2] Yet violence, simulated and real, as (in recent years) in newsreels of the Vietnam war, has been, and is, shown freely daily for universal exhibition in cinemas and on television screens. As I prepare this book for

[2] Robin Wood, *The Times Educational Supplement*, 17.12.76. In a fascinating subsequent article ('Return of the Repressed', 31.12.76) Robin Wood associates sexual repression with devil-worship, horror, extreme violence and a desire for the end of the world as we know it.

press at the time of Christ's nativity, our toy-shop windows, more than ever before in memory, loom large with enormous toy tanks, machine-guns, missile-launchers, toy military men with all the hideous paraphernalia of modern warfare, and children's games which are about obliteration bombing and 'picking off enemy snipers in exposed positions'. I have just seen a radio-controlled tank 'suitable for children from the age of 6'(!) It is now difficult in some shops to buy a portable radio or cassette-recorder which has not been developed, according to current taste, in military style, as if even our listening had to take place on a battlefield. War comics with vivid colours portraying bayonetting and shooting and men with faces like wild beasts are displayed in almost every newsagents (while police and purity campaigners occupy themselves entirely with sex books). Histories of warfare and of weapons, and subscription libraries about warfare and only about warfare, have suddenly mushroomed from nowhere. (From whence?) Presumably all this is done in good faith, or at worst for solid commercial reasons, yet if a war party, solidly in control, were preparing us all for Armageddon it could hardly do better. Again the total war mentality represented in Orwell's *Nineteen Eighty-Four* is closely paralleled.

At Christmas, 1976, the television people did it again. One television authority restricted the season of peace and goodwill to peaceable items in the main, one or two violent gangster films and a film about Pearl Harbour apart: but heralded the new year with feature programmes about the last war in Britain and about warships in the Far East. The other authority celebrated the birthday of Jesus in a truly remarkable way. Christmas night was occupied with *Waterloo*, a two-and-a-half-hour film which includes an hour-long battle scene. Later in the Christmas season we had, on New Year's Day, a long film (almost three hours), at peak time, about General Patton; also *Zulu* ('rank after rank of the last defenders pour leadened defiance at the Zulus from a few yards' range');[3] *From Russia With Love*; *The Finest Hours*; and an edition of *Magpie*, for children, about an assault course for junior guardsmen. This last feature was dealt with, full-page, in the programme magazine under the

[3] *T.V. Times*, 24.12.76

heading 'Family Scene', illustrating a bayonet charge. This list is not an exhaustive one. It should be remembered that throughout this season children were watching at variable hours while on holiday.

One despairs of the hideous ironies revealed in all these things and of the failure of education and religion to do or say anything about them. No doubt these programmes are prepared and presented by honest and reasonable men. The effect, however, is to leave sexuality in a sniggering limbo while presenting violence and war as normal and possibly necessary. No one wants to reduce films and television to sentimental fairy-tales and little else, nor can anyone object to the good old cowboy man-to-man stuff which, in moderation, young people have always enjoyed pretty harmlessly; nor would one want to cut down or ban all films about war, some of which carry a strong anti-war message. But the tasteless torrent of what is, by implication, mass impersonal violence for its own sake is a different thing altogether. The war party, which exists in most major countries, must be absolutely delighted. And if we in education have nothing to do with education for humanity, well and good. But if we have, then our silence about the question of protecting and warning people, and about democratic pressure for legislation—and the silence of the Churches also—would seem to justify one reaction, above all—a dirty laugh. After all, the thing at stake may be the survival of the world.

You cannot have it both ways. If you accept the smashed-in mouth, the bullet-riddled stomach and the terror of mass bombing as standard fare, you should also accept erotic love without reservation, deviant or otherwise, as well. If you ban eroticism, you should ban mindless and insensitive non-touching violence as well, as more extreme even than sexual violence: the censor should then confine both *genres* to private clubs under special licence. Alternatively, we should give the presentation of love the freedom given to the presentation of violence, and let the people choose.

And if schools, and church synods, and women's movements mean business, about caring for young people, they should turn aside from their usual agendas once in a while to bombard Members of Parliament with demands for legislation: to consider the banning of violent films and television shows: to ban war toys of the fearful, modern sophisticated variety and the publicity which goes with them: to ban irresponsible journalism which profits from war; to proscribe these things as surely as racism has been proscribed by law—the issue is no less serious. At present we are brainwashing a whole generation with the cult of war.[4]

[4] Christmas, 1977—the pattern persisted amazingly, BBC television gave people, on the whole, good family entertainment (Marx Brothers, *The Wizard of Oz, National Velvet, Funny Girl,* and a sensitive film about a boy's relationship with an abandoned animal). Independent television provided *How The West Was Won* on Christmas Eve; on Christmas night itself, three hours, almost, of *Young Winston*; and throughout Boxing Day afternoon, when millions of children were dependent on television, three hours, almost, of *The Guns of Navarone.* Three or four other war films followed on this channel during the Christmas Holiday season.

CHAPTER 4

The Fabric of Ordinary Life: A Time for Criticism—Three Sample Studies

In a book which pleads for less puritanism and more pleasure any attack on a common source of pleasure could seem inappropriate. We deceive our pupils as much by our silence about routine habits and diversions, including some pleasures, as about the environment in which we live. Some pleasures highly profitable to their promoters deserve tougher scrutiny than is customary. Here, three, not normally regarded as educational material, are looked at. They could stand as sample studies suitable for every senior school.

1. Smoking

The facts are pretty well known now, and they break down into two major areas: promotion, and its human cost.

In a House of Lords debate[1] we were given the details of sales promotion: the fantastic figure of £70 million spent by tobacco companies in Britain during one year in order to persuade us to smoke—£15,500,000 on advertising in the press, on posters and in cinemas, £50 million on gift coupon schemes, and £2 million to £4 million on other types of promotion.

Less than £500,000 was spent in the same period by H.M. government on health education.

It could be noted here that much of the world's surface utilized for tobacco-growing could more usefully be employed to grow food.

In terms of the obvious human cost: 50,000 people dead in one year in this country alone as a result of tobacco-borne diseases—lung cancer (30,000), chronic bronchitis (a most depressing and debilitating disease) (10,000), emphysema and heart disease attributable to smoking (10,000). About half these casualties are of people in middle life, so that smoking emerges as the biggest preventable cause of death in

[1] 12.5.75

40

the middle-age group, whereas the car is the biggest killer of young people. If a thousand people died each week because of preventable neglect on the railways, or in factories, matters would be put right at once.[2]

If education is about survival, and also about satisfactory living, as I believe it to be, it would seem that young people should be invited as a matter of high priority to consider and talk about the following:

(*i*) *The statistics, especially those directly applicable to children*: smoking harms the unborn child and *kills* a significant number of unborn children each year. (Anti-abortionists do not seem to be bothered about this, in spite of the fact that in this case it is not merely a matter of the first weeks of pregnancy.) Perhaps somewhere in the class discussing these matters is a child whose young brother or sister has been denied life because of this habit.

> One important study shows that at the age of seven the children of mothers who smoked heavily in pregnancy were slightly shorter and four months retarded in reading compared to the children of non-smoking mothers. . . .
> All the British evidence goes to show that smoking cigarettes has a direct influence on the unborn child and is responsible for a higher rate of miscarriages, still-births and early deaths in the children of smoking mothers than in non-smoking mothers. . . .
> The growth of the baby is slowed. Everyone knows that very small babies whether premature or not are at greater risk of dying before or around birth and need special care in premature baby units, and smoking may cause the baby to fall into this category. . . .
> There is evidence that children who come from families of smokers suffer more respiratory disease than those who come from families of non-smokers.[3]

Any sensible un-brainwashed child of 10 or over (and we adults have all been brainwashed) would know how to react to evidence of this sort—with rage and pity.

[2] Later reports (Imperial Cancer Research Fund, 1976) suggest that under the age of 70 smokers run twice the normal risk of death: many more diseases are linked with smoking: a sharper health warning on cigarette packets is called for, and a total smoking ban in cinemas and theatres.

[3] Alfred Yarrow, *So Now You Know about Smoking*, British Medical Association (Family Doctor Booklet), p. 16

(*ii*) *The anomalies.* Drug-taking is heavily frowned on in schools, and grave and earnest talks are given to school-children on this subject. Of course everyone should oppose the use of 'hard' drugs such as heroin and should oppose the spread of other common drugs used in medical practice when they come illegally and dangerously into the hands of children. Perhaps the same should be said about 'soft' drugs (cannabis, or marijuana), though Dr Benjamin Spock now concludes that '... it seems clear to me that marijuana is a drug that is much, much less harmful than heroin, the amphetamines, the barbituates, LSD, alcohol and tobacco.'[4]

The following is an account of the experiences of a television writer's wife who gave up smoking after her husband had compiled a documentary film about a man dying of lung cancer.

> It has been a difficult time at home for us both ... Sue has been going through painful withdrawal symptoms—as a deep inhaler she was totally dependent on nicotine. It got to the point the other week when the irritation of being without her cigarettes got the better of her and she hurled a salad bowl at me, smashing it in the process. But she is determined to stick it out, to win through this time.[5]

What is remarkable about this account is that it candidly describes straight drug addiction, as awful and as compelling as addiction to other drugs now illegal. It is odd that a woman may be fined (and was in court recently) for inadvertently growing a cannabis plant from a packet of bird-seed—or so she convincingly claimed. A man possessing and smoking cannabis to assist him to relax after shift-work was fined £75, which is much more than the fine for many serious motoring offences which could involve hazards to the lives of other people. Yet tobacco-smoking is still normal, even in school staff-rooms and at college and university, on films and in television. Some clergy smoke, and in public. How mad can you get?

(*iii*) *The discourtesy.* There is now medical evidence about the harmful effect of tobacco smoke on the health of non-smokers. The non-smoker may reasonably claim that other

[4] Benjamin Spock, *Bringing up Children in a Difficult Time*, Bodley Head, xxviii, p. 183
[5] *T.V.Times*, 29.3.75, p. 24

people's freedom to pollute the air ends where his nose (his lungs, his skin, his clothes) begin. In fact, the non-smoker loses almost all along the line, in restaurants, in most cinemas, public meetings, single-deck buses. He prefers clean air but he is just smoked over without being consulted. Other people make *him* smell. Education should be about courtesy and concern for others. (Who was the compassionate, amusing and wise man who said, 'Cigarette-smoking is an anti-social act to be entered upon only between consenting adults in private'?)

(iv) The financial reasons. This killing and damaging habit is encouraged because people are making a lot of money out of it and because it brings in millions of pounds in taxation. Here we have an excellent example for discussion of the clash between the needs of people and the needs of institutions. How far are people being sacrificed to institutions? School-children should be asked to consider the moral aspects of this situation.

(v) Deviousness. Education for survival means awareness of how matters are being manipulated. Why should there be the disparity between the official condemnation of cannabis and of tobacco?[6] Do the tobacco producers see the rival drug as a threat? Is cannabis also seen as a threat to our competitive society, because it encourages mental states which do not fit competitive attitudes? To ask questions like this is not to condone the use of cannabis. But we have to help people to ask why tobacco is singled out, like alcohol, as an acceptable drug. Why is tobacco advertising so misleading in its association of smoking with various aspects of the good life? Why is there such a faintness, a slowness to act, about tobacco addiction, in government circles? Are there concealed financial reasons for this? Why does the government not set up, as a matter of urgency, everywhere, free anti-smoking clinics, just as they would set up vaccination clinics if there were an outbreak of smallpox? At present no one is helped very much; one wonders why!

The tobacco affair is a marvellous example, because of our supine acceptance of it, of the inertia encouraged by

---

[6] 'Most of these [in jail] are young people. Some of them are serving terms of twenty and forty years just for possession of marijuana. Sale is punishable by death in one state'—Spock, op. cit., p. 184

education. Every school-child needs mental vaccination against smoking as a contribution to his education for survival. He also needs mental vaccination against being taken in by political mumbo-jumbo. It must be made clear that this is not a process to deprive him of pleasure but to help him to live longer and more healthily and so more enjoyably. It is pathetic that we leave children with so little natural dignity that they can only feel themselves to be 'big' by smoking. And their indulgence in this habit indicates our own failure to give them that buoyant sense of the graciousness and sacramentality of the body, and pride in its efficiency, which would make them want to preserve themselves unpolluted. Nor have we given them enough, as we have driven them sheep-like through formal syllabuses and formal examinations, of that healthy individuality, and doubt of dull conformity, which could help them to be creatively different, instead of one of the mob. It is not without point that the tobacco salesmen in their advertising stand out against individuality. 'Everybody's doing it', they say. 'People like you are smoking our fags.'

2. Animals
The Biblical injunction about God setting man in dominion over all other living things has led to some strange developments:

> 5 hens—each with a wing span of 31 inches—can be kept in a cage 20 inches wide . . .
> A pregnant sow can be kept in a stall barely bigger than herself on concrete without straw—unable to turn. A calf can be confined in a narrow pen in semi-darkness unable to turn round for months on end.[7]

Three books published in recent years should be compulsory reading for all pupils before they leave school, *Savage Luxury* by Brian Davies,[8] Monica Hutchings' and Mavis Caver's *Man's Dominion*,[9] and Ruth Harrison's *Animal Machines*.[10] Together these books deal with factory-farming, seal-hunting, the hunting of the fox, stag, badger and otter,

[7] R.S.P.C.A. Advertisement
[8] Souvenir Press 1970
[9] Rupert Hart-Davies 1970
[10] Vincent Stuart 1964

the life of circus animals, and bull-fighting; and man's elimination of rare species.

It may be asked—What has all this to do with the lecture-
room or classroom? There are firm links with general education. The traffic in animal cruelty is part of the money-
system about which our pupils are not adequately aware. As
in the case of the tobacco industry, the suffering and the
killing must go on because they pay well. Furthermore, animals form a vital part of the environment. Therefore any
cohesive view of nature should include not only sympathy for
all living things, but also an intelligent awareness of nature's
balance, and of the part which plants and animals and trees
play in the vital life-cycle on which our own existence
depends. Thirdly, if we desensitize ourselves concerning animals, we ultimately make ourselves callous about our
fellow-men. American soldiers training to fight in Vietnam
were prepared psychologically to view the Vietnamese as
'mere animals', so that American soldiers could exterminate
the Vietcong without conscience by any means available. A
famous *Guardian* cartoon dating from the early days of
factory-farming made the same point in another way. It
showed six views of a chicken hanging upside down on a
conveyor belt in a battery farm helplessly awaiting slaughter.
The face in the first frame was simply that of a hen, but it
changed as the pictures went on, until in the sixth picture it
was the face of a man. 'How big a step is it from the broiler-
house to Auschwitz?' asked the *Guardian*. We and our pupils
are educated not to ask questions like that one. We are not
supposed to ask how our veal has been prepared, how our
eggs are produced, our milk, our bacon; how much or how
little the animals we enjoy at the circus and at the zoo have
suffered for our pleasure; how the musk for some of our
perfume has been prepared (by whipping or provoking the
Abyssinian civet cat; the animals are kept in cages so small
that they often cannot turn round, and the musk is scraped
from them every ten days).

The whole matter is also essentially one of government, an
appropriate area for education. The Brambell Report on
factory-farming produced in 1969 under the distinguished
chairmanship of Professor F. W. Rodgers Brambell was
deliberately watered down in practice. Dr Brambell himself

wrote to *The Times* under the heading 'Codes for Factory Farming: Rules without Force'.[11]

One wonders what baleful influences were brought to bear on government agencies. One wonders how often such influences are brought to bear. Another correspondent in *The Times* was more direct than Professor Brambell: 'It is well known that barbarians cared for their flocks and herds with skill and compassion. The opposite is true of the Civil Servants responsible for the Draft Codes.'[12]

What kind of people are ruling us? As I write, a current example is the permitting of smoking experiments applied to captive beagles, which are compelled to inhale tobacco smoke until they become ill, in the interests of research for a safer cigarette—not even in the interests of something perhaps more pressing, such as cancer research. One survey suggests that two-thirds of the people interviewed wished these tests to be abandoned. But there is a profounder question than a mere expression of public opinion. Are we, *homo sapiens*, really worth it all? Do *our* lives, mean, conformist, gossipy and money-grubbing, really justify all this misery to other living creatures? I doubt it.

If we wish to have a more humane world we have to help pupils to realize their role in this. Therefore they should be faced squarely and unsentimentally with the cost, in terms of pain and deprivation, of our so-called civilization; and they should debate vivisection and vegetarianism and be allowed to make up their own minds as to moral priorities. But when suffering without due reason, for profit or trivial pleasure, is involved, it is part of our duty to express utter abhorrence, and to recruit sympathy from young people before they are made cynical. How should a child react when—on his way to school assembly, with its sugary hymns—he sees a lorry loaded with hundreds of tiny crates, into which live hens have been pushed so tightly that they are half-asphyxiated, cannot move without injuring one another, and where some have wing-feathers broken? How does a baby elephant feel when it is taken from its herd and handed over to a circus after a long and terrifying journey, much of it in semi-darkness? And how would its mother feel? What bearing should these thoughts

[11] 1.7.69
[12] 1.7.69

have on visits to zoos, and circuses, and to some animal films? Since politicians are lethargic, it seems that only education could spearhead an attack on all unnecessary animal suffering. Here is a fertile area for children to write, talk, act, paint and draw—and learn how to organize decent and orderly protest. We are being unfair to our pupils if we do not help them to realize their own full humanity in defence of other living things. The Churches, as so often about things that are real, are largely silent. The Bishop of Winchester, John Taylor, gives us one of the rarely-heard effective comments in his excellent book, *Enough is Enough*.[13] It has been estimated that

out of 500,000,000 animals slaughtered every year throughout the world, only about eleven per cent—55,000,000—are killed humanely. . . .[14]

Rightly or wrongly, I hate the idea of keeping hens in those wire chests of drawers they call batteries. I think it is cruel and also that it produces an inferior article of food. It is no good telling me that they wouldn't thrive if they were unhappy. The time when I really put on weight was when I sat in trenches for a year, dirty, wet, frightened and miserable.[15]

I cringe every time I see the club starting to swing down on those defenceless animals, and when the blood spurts over the ice. . . . Many baby seals were being skinned alive and it was heartbreaking watching the mothers trying to protect their babies. . . . On average, 400,000 seals are killed annually for the Canadian and Norwegian markets. . . . [Brian Davies] added that the book also showed up the Canadian Government in a very bad light. It describes the tactics which industry and government will use to block any changes that essentially cost them money. . . . There have been some improvements over the past few years. . . . If the young girls who wear fur coats were aware of the enormous suffering that went into creating the coats, they would strip them off their backs and burn them immediately.[16]

Fortunately children sometimes seize upon the reality and

[13] John V. Taylor, *Enough is Enough*, S.C.M. Press 1975 (see Chapter 2)
[14] *Sun*, 16.1.70
[15] Laurence Easterbrook, quoted by Ruth Harrison in *Animal Machines*
[16] Clare Good in a review of *Savage Luxury*, *Sun*, 26.9.70

practicality which the official moralists miss. Let's end with a word of hope from Brian Davies

> ... [he] spoke of a touching letter he had received from a 12-year-old schoolgirl in answer to an appeal for funds against seal-hunting. He told me, 'She had gone out into the street with her school note-book and had collected pennies and signatures from people. Altogether she raised £2 for the cause. I was very moved by her letter.'[17]

3. Movement[18]

'How do you know,' says Blake, 'but ev'ry Bird that cuts the airy way, Is an immense world of delight, clos'd by your senses five.'

The goodness of creative movement is an 'in' thing in schools, and a more sensitive aesthetic has revolutionized Physical Education since the days of 'drill'. It is a pity, therefore, that young people are growing up in a world in which the simple business of moving about the face of the Earth has become so unpleasant, and that we do nothing to alert them to it, or to change it.

The facts are emotive and at the same time clinical; and they touch every child in every school, and every student in higher education. Car crashes, reports the World Health Organization, are the biggest killers of young men in Europe. In West Germany more than half the deaths of young men occur on the roads, in Scotland a third, in England and Wales 42 per cent. The biggest cause of death in Ulster during 1973 was not terrorism—but road accidents; the mortality figures exceeded deaths due to terrorism by almost a hundred. In York and North-East Yorkshire road deaths doubled between October 1971 and October 1972. During 1971 a quarter of a million people died on the world's roads and 7,500,000 were injured. '*Spectacularly at risk*, especially in technically-developed countries, are adolescent and adult males between 15 and 24 years old' (my italics).[19]

One would have thought that statistics like these brought

[17] Ibid

[18] Written before the massive fare increases and unprecedented cuts in rail services proposed in 1976–7: these are certain to result in substantially-increased profits for all concerned with road transport and a substantial increase in road deaths.

[19] T. E. A. Benjamin, 'Safety and the Driver', *The Times*, 5.10.73

road travel firmly into the purview of education—even if one omitted the all-too-frequent, emotive headlines: the boy of 7 in hospital who is not to be told that his entire family has been wiped out in a car crash; 'Father finds son dead in crash'; 'Catastrophic injuries in a road crash turned him from a lively and bright little boy into a human wreck'; 'Readers are asked to remember in their prayers our son and daughter-in-law, who have had a second son killed in a road accident'. And so on. Sometimes it seems that in education we fail to touch upon real issues either with figures or with feelings.

And the non-human price? In 1961 the cost to the nation of each fatal casualty was £2,970, for each serious casualty £770, for each slight casualty £50.[20] The total cost of road accidents each year even in the early 1960s was estimated, including damage to vehicles and property and administrative costs, to be in the region of £170 million.[21] It has disturbingly been estimated that of young children now at school, at least one in every two will be involved in a road accident at some time in their lives.

If one thinks of all this as directly applicable to the young people we teach, it begins to sink in, but as the editor of *The Listener* once said, 'Cars—in this and other matters—have brought about a slow but deadly attrition of our sense of what is rational and acceptable.'[22] This, in terms of communication or lack of it, is vital educational material. Dr John Moorman, Bishop of Ripon, says,

> If on the front page of the *Yorkshire Post* this morning you read of a train smash in which 20 people have been killed and many hundreds injured, you would be horrified. If you read of similar smashes every day for a week or a month or a year there would be an outcry. No one would travel by train. There would be questions in Parliament, angry leaders in the newspapers, public inquiries and so on. Yet the equivalent of this in human misery happens every day. We know about it. We deplore it. But it has been going on so long that we have learnt to live with it, and perhaps we don't give it much thought.[23]

[20] More recent (1976) figures, issued, for example, by Humberside Police, give the cost of each fatal accident as £44,400, and the annual cost to each ratepayer of all accidents as £10 per head. These figures, and others like them, are not mentioned when governments publicize economy drives.

[21] John Davey, 'How to Stop the Killing', *Observer*, 17.4.66

[22] *The Listener*, 16.6.66., p. 864

[23] John Moorman, 'Death on the Roads', *Yorkshire Post*, 4.6.66

Dr Moorman's comments go cheek by jowl with a column devoted to the details of anthems and other rituals in various cathedrals. One feels that his comments are at least as useful as a contribution to the Kingdom of God as the more comfortable doings described nearby. In a similar spirit Dr Gerald Ellison, Bishop of Chester and President of the Pedestrians' Association, has said that the public has become 'punch drunk' about accident figures.

All we get in our schools and colleges are (within their limits very excellent and life-saving) safety talks and demonstrations by police and (at some colleges) compulsory driving instruction. The deeper questions, as usual, are not asked, and our life-style not questioned, even though hundreds of young lives are at risk. On this inescapable and simple question of human movement, every pupil before leaving school should be invited to talk over matters like the following: they are essential to his education: they are either broadly factual or broadly moral.

A. Factual

Statistics—the accident details like those above (by no means well known).[24] Absolutely vital educational material for the assessing of life-style.

Communication—an in-word in education, but in this vital matter we are not communicating, just as the newspaper reports of road accidents do not adequately communicate the shock, distress, bereavement.

The obvious pressures at work upon us. The car has been glamorized to the tune of millions. People have been invited to 'Have a love affair' with 'the car in your life'. Cars are used to advertise other things, and other things are used to 'push' cars. Cars are increasingly brash, garishly-coloured, psuedo-romantic; through advertising the car has been linked with the good, sexual, affluent life, and as a method of getting away to lonely, unspoilt places—which the car is spoiling or has already spoilt. It is worth juxtaposing the persuasive advertisements with the reality of car crashes—like those portrayed in Godard's film, 'Weekend'.

Pupils should also be made aware of pressure groups other

[24] *Guardian* reprinted article, 'Statistic' (1963), reproduced in quantity for educational purposes, provides an effective educational instrument.

than the car manufacturers. The Road Haulage Association, which has its own education section, and its constituent parts, which include the A.A. and R.A.C.; and the Road Campaign Council, which was asking as long ago as 1966 for a road-building programme costing £7,100,000,000 to give Britain 2,700 miles of motorway by 1980—these should be known. The Road Campaign Council's 1966 report asked for road development even at the cost of temporary reductions in investment in other social services. Its recommendations included much more than doubling the then motorway programme and the construction of a primary network of urban motorways in all large and medium-sized towns; also the provision of an extra million parking spaces. These recommendations were supported by the County Surveyors' Society.

The environmental case. Arguments like those immediately above should be considered in relation to the 66,000 acres of Britain disappearing annually under concrete, and with the disturbance and destruction of wild life resulting from the road-building programme.

B. Moral

A number of less obvious but interesting matters fall into the moral or ideological field. They exhibit contradictory features, failures to connect, a kind of moral and verbal schizophrenia to which we should alert our young citizens.

(a) *Aggression and helplessness.* The car has made people more aggressive. Gone are the courteous days when motorists helped one another and respected the public at large. Motorways and trunk roads, with their slip-roads which can only be used aggressively and at speed, are helping to produce a race which gives and expects no quarter. The barbarous and warlike names given to cars underline this characteristic. Indeed, increasingly car design suggests either the rocket or the tank. The world requires research into the genetic damage done by the car in encouraging the production of edgy, aggressive people.

It is very amusing, therefore, that this domineering and aggressive thing has produced, at bureaucratic levels, a kind of baby-like helplessness. It is helplessly assumed by governments that cars and lorries (and pollution and wastage of

the Earth's surface, and deaths) must go on multiplying themselves year after year, like steel beetles, at if Man were helpless to stop them. One wonders how authority would react if
we were confronted with a plague of cats, or birds. Says the
New Statesman:

> While we hopefully debate ways of curtailing the rise of the
> population of India, we accept as an inevitable forecast that there
> will be 18,000,000 cars on the British roads in 1980, as if they
> were generated by an uncontrollable reproductive urge. The
> motor industry is not really so vital to the economy, nor even to
> the level of exports, as is often believed; less than 3 per cent of the
> national income arises from the production of cars. But the real
> necessities, which we are in danger of losing, are cities and towns
> which function efficiently and in which life is tolerable, and the
> countryside in a fit state to be enjoyed. Ceaselessly the cars roll
> off the assembly lines. But improvement in public transport
> comes about far more slowly. . . .[25]

Again it is supinely accepted that the legal speed limits
cannot be enforced—indeed everyone knows that they are
ignored a million times each day. About a 'killer' bend near
my own home the Department of the Environment lamely
says that further restrictions are pointless because they would
not be observed. Blame for deaths on the road is petulantly
flung at teachers or parents. A county safety bulletin says,
'The most dangerous action a child can take is to run into the
road'. How true—and how pointless to say this, when the real
enemy is the proliferating car. Officialdom, in supporting this
symbol of power and aggression, reveals itself as powerless or
nearly so. It has, morally, given up.

(b) *Social priorities*. There are schools without paper or
chalk. £520,000,000 was allocated by the government for
road-works in April 1972. No money at all was allocated to
the British Waterways Board in 1973, although environmentalists give that body support. £1,000,000,000 was at one
time the estimated cost for the London Motorway Box
(£1,500,000,000 for the Concorde project). There are hospitals without staff, and school headmasters struggling along
without adequate secretarial help. Recently a young girl
helper fainted because she had been left alone in charge of

[25] 'Civilising the Motor Car', *New Statesman*, 13.5.66

over forty E.S.N. patients in a state geriatric home. Every mile of motorway costs a million pounds. These facts talk, and they should be talked about.

(c) *What people want.* A government survey published in 1974 revealed that two out of ten people were seriously disturbed by traffic, and that more than half wanted traffic banned from more residential roads. The Ramblers Association, defending the public's access to the countryside against the threat of a new road system, said of one scheme: 'We believe that the road plan only displays one of the worst aspects of the planning process today, the insensitivity associated with expediency.'[26] Matters of this sort however are not widely advertised for public debate or for referendum, and favoured groups, rather than the public weal, are awarded the official ear when it comes to official action.

(d) *The credibility gap.* A chairman of a big car firm once remarked that he hoped every family in Britain would soon possess a car. Yet it is obvious in view of the static amount of land in these islands that things would become impossible if this were so.

Even the average school-child can see that the area of land on this Earth, particularly the area of land in the British Isles, is limited. It does not marvellously expand because the head of a car firm waves his magic wand; and there just is not room for every family to have a house to live in, a garden, a car, or several cars, and possibly an extra movable home in the form of a caravan behind the car. This is a selfish and excessive use of space, and if we all claim it life will be intolerable.

But the notion of moral control in this area is a fresh one, and meanwhile cars get bigger all the time. As *The Listener* remarks, the choice is between a tolerable urban and rural environment, or 'two cars in every family used on every possible occasion. Unless we expand the acreage of Britain, We cannot possibly have both.'

(e) *The moral gap.* If the credibility gap reveals a kind of madness, the moral gap points towards a failure in moral communication. It is not that the enthusiastic planners of roads, and the car and the lorry lobbies, have rejected the facts about road casualties: it is simply that, when it comes to

[26] *Guardian,* 8.1.75

the crunch, as the smoker ignores the facts about the dangers of cigarettes, they ignore them. In 1984-like terms of double-think, these facts, for them, do not exist. Individual manufacturers have introduced palliative safety features, although one big American firm has just called for a five-year moratorium, for the sake of economy, on further air pollution and safety measures. But the central facts, that cars kill and roads kill, and that more cars and more roads mean more killing, just has not penetrated the moral consciousness of the more ruthless people in big business, nor of the civil servants who have supervised the closing-down of good, safe railways and have gone, and still daily do so, to very great pains to make sure that public transport is not made too convenient.

One detailed educational study or project which utilizes some of the ideas of this chapter is outlined in Chapter 5 below. It's a project not only about learning lots of facts, a familiar ploy, but also about how to live, and how to survive. That has been the point of the three examples above. Maps of the Brazilian jungle, and test-papers on *Hamlet*, may have substantial educational value. But it is arguable that learning how not to get killed when you are young, how not to kill yourself in middle life, and how not to cause unnecessary suffering to dumb creatures, may be more important.

CHAPTER 5

Criticizing the Social Fabric (2) Projects that Bite

A Railway Project

Statistics about the car compare interestingly with figures about the railways, which are still in slow decline. During a rail go-slow in London there were thirteen more road accidents a day than was normal. Following a rise in petrol prices, road deaths in North and South Yorkshire fell by one-half. On the Isle of Wight two people were killed on railways during 105 years of rail operation, now virtually over. In Britain as a whole casualties in train accidents are now down to about one per million train miles.[1] Statistically it would seem to be irrefutable that every time you close a railway down you kill lots of people. Who bothers? Politics is not about people!

At the lower end of the school where activity is relatively free it is customary for children to engage in interesting studies and projects round centres of interest, often across the inter-disciplinary barriers. These projects are good, and they are fun, though at this level they are usually informative only and cannot go very deep. They often lead to good 'creative' work. Except with non-exam classes, this kind of activity diminishes in secondary and higher education in favour of the more formal methods. This is a pity: because, given social edge, they could lead to some useful social illumination. In the primary school, the wheel, the farm, the canal, the history of flight, the railway—they all come up so often. What about a railway project for older pupils which is really a social instrument, not merely a collection of maps, pictures and historical and scientific data? It might well go something like this:

Pupils would be encouraged, after suitable preparation, and in relation to their own home area, to interview people, to observe and compile statistics, and inspect printed data. They would find, I suspect, a good deal of contrast between the commercial glamorization of the car and the contemporary

[1] During 1976 there were no passenger deaths on Britain's railways.

approach to other forms of transport, and to the train in particular. They would find railway advertising relatively poor. They would find that a hundred years or more of railway achievement, with a tremendous mechanical and architectural history behind it, has been run down progressively over the last thirty or forty years. They would find extensive recent records of the late running of trains, cancellations and breakdowns, to a degree unknown thirty years ago, even under wartime conditions, and not all due to industrial disputes—in the main merely routine. Fares would be found to be high enough to deter some people from travelling at all by train, or from taking their cycles, which at one time it was economical to do. They would find that rail fares rise substantially every time petrol prices rise.[2] They would talk to people, especially older people, and find evidence of difficulties about luggage, and porters, and tickets, and reservations. They would find that timetables often don't 'work'. They would find 'connections' that don't connect, and a great deal of difference between well-publicized attempts to persuade people to use certain main-line trains and a tendency to discourage passengers on branch lines. They might, if they developed the Sherlock Holmes' technique with timetables, unearth subtler things, like British Rail's habit of running the last train of the day on many branch lines at about 2100 hours, when nobody needs it, too late for those wishing to be home for the evening and too early for those who have enjoyed an evening out. They will interview older brothers and sisters at college, and find that weekend travel by rail has been made so difficult and so frustrating that students home for a couple of days rely on 'lifts' or 'hitches'. They will find that trains are no longer duplicated or adequately lengthened at peak times, as they once were, so that many journeys are grossly overcrowded.

They can look back into the newspapers of the 1960s, in the hey-day of the railway closures, and find letters like those quoted in Appendix A.[3] They might begin to notice some very queer things; like the official advice given to passengers undertaking the once very popular rail journey from the

---

[2] Which would be totally inexcusable if the railways had stuck to coal, now abundant again, instead of going over to oil.

[3] See pp. 155–7

densely-populated area of West Yorkshire to the Lake District: that they should get off their train at Carnforth, carry their cases up a hill, and complete the last thirty miles or so by bus. (Although there are railway lines all the way to Windermere there are no longer any convenient connections at Carnforth for that town.) They might notice that a branch line due for closure (and later closed) was given departures of rush-hour trains to the nearest city before 08.00 hours and after 09.00 hours, but nothing at the time of peak demand between 8 and 9. They might come across the case of the rush-hour train in another area which was reduced to two overcrowded coaches, while large, empty trains ran on the same line off-peak. They could take sample cross-country journeys hypothetically taken by parents and friends to see how helpful or otherwise the rail services are.

It would be important to encourage a scrupulous fairness during these investigations, emphasizing that there are many dedicated railwaymen at all levels in the railway hierarchy: that these people do their best under very difficult conditions—conditions typified for example by the Department of the Environment's refusal to find a few thousand pounds to keep a branch line (badly timetabled) open, while finding nearly half a million pounds merely to reconstruct five miles of the hard shoulder on a motorway in Northamptonshire. The Divisional Manager without a reserve train in an emergency may be helpless because he is being denied the reserves which were formerly customary. At the same time, the grotesque and undemocratic nature of the manipulation of public affairs from off-stage in our times can be illustrated from much newspaper correspondence from a complaining public, from reports of Transport Users' Consultative Committee's enquiries, and perhaps in lighter vein with grosser examples from abroad. There were the Pacific coast lines in the U.S.A., which tried to get rid of passengers by stopping all the washing of coach windows; and the scenic train from coast to coast in North America which now goes through the Rockies at night only, so that you can't see anything.

This is all a bit more pointed than the potted railway history we often accept from pupils. The investigation might fall naturally, in due time, into various areas of interest, corresponding to the diverse interests of pupils–

1. Figures

Mathematically-minded pupils can investigate in detail road/rail costs, compare fares by different modes of transport, calculate the percentages of efficient or inefficient running, ask passengers about lateness, defective heaters, over-crowding: compile statistics.

2. Human geography

Pupils can identify areas remote from useful forms of public transport or with inadequate connections to them, with special reference to London and other major cities. In cases where rail connections appear to be good, they should be carefully checked and people interviewed. The function of railways abroad would provide good comparative studies.

3. History, then and now

The Bishop of Winchester, John Taylor, has put this excellently in *Enough is Enough,*

> In the eighteenth century, for example, Britain's incomparable network of canals, developed by such engineering geniuses as James Brindley and Thomas Telford, was the nerve-system of the Industrial Revolution. Birmingham has more miles of canal than Venice. Tunnelled through the hills, lifted on elegant aqueducts above the rivers or on broad embankments over the dry valleys, curving with the contours of the landscape, these waterways were things of great beauty as well as usefulness. One fully-loaded barge today carries the equivalent of five lorries. But then came the railways, and they saw the canals as rivals. In Europe the two systems were seen to be complementary and today the canals of France, Germany, Austria and the Low Countries offer a viable alternative to rail and road for heavy industrial loads. In 1969 237,000,000 tons was waterborne in Holland alone, but less than 7,000,000 in Britain. What happened? The nineteenth-century rail companies in Britain and in the U.S.A. were allowed systematically to buy up the canals, then starve them of trade and neglect their maintenance, until there was no choice but to close them down. A much needed and a very beautiful asset was destroyed for the sake of a new interest that could neither accept limits nor brook rivals. That is what I mean by the mentality of a spoilt child. And now, as a fantastic nemesis of repeated waste, it is the turn of Britain's marvellous rail network to be sacrificed to the jealousy of the next usurper—road transport. Every few years

58

larger regions of Britain are made virtually inaccessible to any but car owners and long-distance juggernauts. The abandonment of thousands of miles of track, with its tunnels, embankments, viaducts and shunting-yards, is a monumental price to pay for the monopoly of a nation's transport . . . the railways indulged in the gigantic throwaway of an efficient canal system and were themselves, in turn, thrown away by the British road transport interests.[4]

This brings emphasis to the point that the sins of the early railway pioneers are being visited on the railways a century later—that commercial rottenness is endemic, and monotonous. Pupils can be helped to see the peculiar ironies in the situation: the serious railway accidents of the early railway years (see Victorian journals), though they were far less damaging to human life than the activities of the lorry and the car today, received much more sensational publicity—now, when the railways, assisted by modern technology, have a superb safety record, they are being demolished in favour of transport with a quite dreadful safety record. It can be pointed out that modern roads, with their streaming and gantries and illuminated signs and elaborate junctions, look more and more like railways, though, with more irony, they lack the safety of the trains. It will also be useful to show the special wrong-headedness of Britain and North America in all this sorry story, and pupils well acquainted with European countries will be able to provide further examples of the selfish commercialism of the U.S.A. and Great Britain in its full lack of social discipline, as compared with the better social priorities of other countries. (Why should these things be? What forces have been brought, in the shadows, to bear?)

4. Social studies
Pupils could investigate the successes and failures of public protests against rail cuts: newspaper correspondence, newspaper articles, and the proceedings of the Transport Users' Consultative Committees set up in the form of public enquiries to debate the closure of lines: interviews with people affected would be very worth while. It would probably be found that some protest movements had been handled courteously by the authorities concerned—others with

[4] Pp. 25–6, 29

brusque lack of courtesy. (I have attended two public enquiries—one courteously dealt with: at the other public protesters were treated with contempt.) Especially likely to appeal to pupils researching here is a letter like that from the York schoolgirls printed in Appendix A.[5] What we are really doing here is not just looking at railways, but harnessing the radical and rebellious spirit of young people. We are demonstrating, meanwhile, that democracy is working, at best, imperfectly.

5. Peripheral matters—including fun

This is all a serious business, but we must help people to laugh at life's absurdities. Some pupils would do best in their contribution to the comic side of things. There are lots of funny railway stories. Jon Akass in the popular *Sun* has championed railways against the car with typical humour, noting the absurdity of destruction disguised as efficiency or as (in railway management terms) 're-shaping'. And in a glorious article in support of the man who walked, on principle, over a car parked on a public footpath, he wrote '. . . it is now time to come off the fence before you are knocked off by a hundred-ton lorry, or have it removed from under you to make way for a clover-leaf flyover. Lorries so big that they judder window panes as they pass, should be taken by Ministry of Transport officials to a suitable piece of waste ground, and put to the flame. The A.A. and the R.A.C. should be disbanded in the public interest.'[6] In contrast there is the tragic irony of the veteran soldier who survived Dunkirk and was killed by a car on his return to Belgium for a reunion pilgrimage thirty-five years later.

Certainly other transport services will come under scrutiny, and it may be found that many bus services are uncoordinated and inconvenient, while others are very good. It would be useful to find whether smaller private companies serve the public better, or less efficiently, than larger groups like the National Bus Company. It would also be instructive to discover how easy it is, or how difficult, to secure bus and rail timetables. (In my own area of Yorkshire they are often out of print. Although valiant efforts are now being made to provide

[5] See pp. 155–6

[6] Jon Akass, 'Let's All Run Over Cars For A Change', *Sun*, 27.9.72

convenient buses into the Yorkshire Dales on summer weekends, routine bus services from West Yorkshire cities into Yorkshire's beauty spots, and the corresponding rail arrival and departure times, seem designed to discourage people. In so many cases they 'just miss'.)

Pupils should interview foreign visitors:

> 'I am very impressed by public transport in your city', he told me. 'You have elaborate services to the suburbs, and there are also frequent trains to London. . . . We have no bus services in our community . . . we estimate that everyone has a car and therefore public transport is not needed.' . . .
>
> Apparently there are occasional buses to Syracuse, but that is all. No passenger trains. . . .
>
> Professor Sternlicht, Professor of English at New York State University, regretted the motor age. He described the car as 'an anti-social piece of machinery which will eventually choke your cities to death'. . . .
>
> Unfortunately Britain had not profited by America's experience. We were still building wider and longer roads, which could only become more crowded over the years. The whole process was self-defeating. . . .
>
> He thought that eventually public transport systems would reassert themselves. Even the railway tracks which were now being torn up might have to be re-laid.[7]

This was reported of an American visitor to York at the height of the railway closures of the 1960s.

There is fine material in all this for researching in newspapers and magazines, for cutting things out and pasting them up and grouping them, and for geography and history and social studies which are really practical, as well as for *practical* moral education.

Conclusions

Students are likely to draw conclusions and gain educational experience from a project like this in a variety of ways. For some, fairly traditional forms of achievement will suffice: graphs and statistics, creative writing in prose or verse, painting and drawing. The movement out towards new forms of educational experience will begin when the artist learns to

[7] John Blunt, 'York's Public Transport is Impressive, Says U.S. Don', *Yorkshire Evening Press,* 9.6.66

compare his drawing of the large, three-quarters-empty main-line station, echoing and under-used, with the jammed road outside; when the whizz-kid who loves figures digs out some of the more eccentric *non-sequiturs* from the timetables, and chats with parents and friends about different conditions years ago. The historical and geographical aspects are obvious, but equally valuable will be the questions raised in terms of a study in democracy—to make us ask questions. For example—Who rules the country? Who has done all this? Who is really better for it? What has been and still is, every single day, the real cost in human suffering? Beyond all this, the work will be an essay in human movement about the Earth, movement which has been made so nasty and brutish and perhaps too dangerous to use. The ablest pupils will go deep into social history, disinterring perhaps some of the startling facts available in the files of the relevant trade union.[8] Perhaps our brightest boy or girl, after a browse through the book-shops, will shock and entertain us with a summary of the story in miniature told in *The Great Isle of Wight Train Robbery*,[9] an astonishing tale of wheeler-dealing, lies, duplicity and evasion, at all levels, in response to democratic and civilized public protest. As usual, 'the pale pathetic peoples' were defeated. And how much more useful would all this be than the dreary 'précis' of the average 'O'-level paper?

[8] See Appendix B, pp. 160–2
[9] R. E. Burroughs, *The Great Isle of Wight Train Robbery,* Railway Invigoration Society 1969

CHAPTER 6

Peace and the People

The leader of Britain's university dons warned today that, while
£450m. is being spent on improving Polaris missiles, the universities are suffering savagely from economy cuts. . . .
   Prof. David King, president of the 29,000-strong Association
of University Teachers, said . . . 'the Government is still able to
spend £450m.—or nearly four-fifths of the total annual grant to
universities—on a programme to "improve" the nuclear warhead
for the Polaris missiles, an improvement described by experts as
minimal.'[1]

This book was written, in part, during one of the world's
wretched and recurring international crises. While military
forces gathered and there was open discourse about retali-
ation with, or even about the pre-emptive use of, the nuclear
bomb, the separate world of school and of higher education
operated in its usual protected manner, occupied with its own
artificial internal tensions, mark-sheets, timetables. There
was something obscene about this uncaring separateness. After
all, we are, in the education service, reputed to be concerned
with the welfare of young people, whose predicament under
nuclear bombardment is intolerable to think of.

   But in our worship of objective truth we distance ourselves
from sympathetic reality. Though supposed to be concerned
and caring people, we have nothing to say about the movement towards a fearful war in which children will be the worst
sufferers. That cold, cerebral quality, which we believe to be
the same as the disinterested search for knowledge, kills our
generous emotive responses.

   Again we ask—'Whom shall we send, and who will go for
us?' A frail United Nations Organization tries to hold the
world together by voluntary agreement, while diplomats, with
great knowledge and skill, usually manage to get us through a
crisis, but seem unable to change attitudes and structures
needful for the prevention of crises.

[1] *Yorkshire Evening Press,* December, 1976

The need is for education in world government. And that means a reconsideration of teaching about sovereignty, about the hidden reasons for man's failure to achieve peace, and about the education of politicians.

Sovereignty in its old forms is an out-moded concept. C. E. M. Joad, just after the Second World War, and with his eye upon the new dangers then facing us, described the modern nation-state as obsolescent. No one should try to discredit genuine patriotism in schools. But 'New occasions teach new duties'. The true patriot, in pre-nuclear days, may have been justified in sticking firmly to the notion of his country's total independence—though independent patriotism of this kind has often been buccaneering and the cause of much violence and conquest. Nowadays the old-fashioned patriot can bring about the destruction of his own country if he fails to see his nation as one knit—whether he likes it or not—within an interdependent fellowship of nations. With the hydrogen bomb as an uncomfortable neighbour we can't go it alone any more. The old game of doing as one likes is over. Joad was right. The spirit of Shakespeare's *Henry V* (and that marvellous and moving play includes in its action, be it noted, a barely-justified attack upon France) has to make way for the reconciling spirit of the later Shakespeare, perhaps particularly of *Cymbeline,* in which Britain and her old enemies join together in fraternity, and flags 'wave together'.

No one wants a monolithic world in which all national differences have been swallowed up. Old-fashioned patriots always reject the idea of world federalism because they confuse it with the monolithic, super-state model. But they forget two things—first, that unless we achieve some sort of *binding* world order, as in the running of a company, or a school, or a family, we may be left with little more than a blackened, empty planet savaged by nuclear war. If there were survivors from such a war—and this would be doubtful—they would face a terrible, near-total dictatorship needful for the reestablishment of order—a necessary tyranny far worse than *any* kind of world government peacefully-achieved. For that peaceful achievement some degree of surrender of sovereignty is essential.

The second reply to the old-fashioned enthusiast for sovereignty at all costs is the reminder that a peacefully-

achieved world federation would not mean the elimination of
the best elements in nationhood. But it would take away the
dangerous elements. When a nation surrenders its armed
forces to a central, international police force, when it surrenders some degree of control over currency and trade, it
does not surrender everything. It does not surrender customs,
local laws and by-laws, ethnic differences—nor does it lose
that intense and very local patriotism for towns and regions,
which is often much more real than artifically-heightened
national pride. Moreover, a new power is gained by the electorate, because each citizen possesses, under federal government, a double vote. A British citizen under a world
federal government would still elect national representatives for purely national affairs in Britain to a British
parliament, but he would also elect representatives to a
world parliament. The federations we already have—the
U.S.A., Switzerland, amongst others—imperfect, and variable in style as they may be, prove their workability. With
the E.E.C. firmly established, perhaps the next step is to
federate Europe. This would be one step towards ultimate
world government.

The choice is no longer one between proud, competing
national sovereignties and one world order, but between one
world order and chaos. The federal idea was much noised
abroad immediately after the Second World War and has
since, for a variety of reasons, been quietly shelved. It is
always being dismissed as impractical and sentimental. Yet
the strange fact is that it enshrines an idea of order, of men
just not doing exactly as they please, already taken for
granted in every civilized village, town, city in the world,
though not at the world level, *where it is most desperately
wanted.* We need new risks of trust, and an end to the brink-
manship which has marked the post-war era. Compared with
the monstrous possibility of world destruction, the suggestion
that we pool the armed forces of the super-powers for the sake
of peace seems relatively sensible, relatively moderate. Fantastic though it may seem, our only final hope *vis à vis* our
principal world adversaries lies in federating with them (see
Cymbeline again—how true is art!). Such a step would be
opposed all the way by those who make, and glory in, military
weapons, and is already so opposed, and effectively so. But it

would also be opposed by officials, quite sincere people, who just have not begun to understand.

Amazing though the admission may be, we do not teach sane world government in schools. The omission is lamentable in the extreme, almost the worst of the many gloomy gaps left in the threadbare educational scene. Since there are many reasons, most of them nasty, for the world's failure to secure world government, the role of education familiarly resembles the role of pimp, or prostitute, to evil. It agrees, in its silence, with the intents of the dark forces which intend us never to have peace.

We live in apocalyptic times. Only tremendous and generous stretches of imagination can save us. If anyone doubts the fantastic nature of our times let him recall events following upon the murder of President Jack Kennedy, who was almost certainly killed because he had begun to secure firm agreements with Russia and because he was suspected of wishing to withdraw American forces from South-East Asia. Eighteen material witnesses involved in the Warren Commission which investigated his assassination have died from various causes in the three years following their giving of evidence. The odds against all this having happened by chance have been estimated to be in the trillion rather than the billion bracket. We are faced, world-wide, with a vast arms conspiracy, about which young people are told nothing. Even our moderate *Radio Times*, commenting on John Maddox's programme, *Will the Bomb Spread?* said:

> What are the prospects for the proliferation of nuclear weapons among the potential nuclear powers? Have the established super-powers met their side of the bargain by their attempt to reduce nuclear strategic arms, or will they or should they? Will the commercial pressures for selling nuclear equipment undermine the nuclear non-proliferation system?[2]

How incredible a world! That something as critical as control of deadly weapons possessing the power to destroy the world should be at the whim of money, sheer money!

It is, as it is with the pollution of the environment, with transport, with the commercial exploitation of animals and of man's leisure—a financial gamble, with ourselves as the

[2] *Radio Times*, 29.5.75

baubles. For this reason does the Pentagon, whenever military estimates come up for review, frighten the American people and the West in general, with loud talk about defence gaps, so that the millions and the billions may go on being spent on things designed to kill, so that the manic spiral of fear and tension will go on.

The factor which seems to be missing in the discourse about war, the factor so surprisingly absent from the talk of diplomats and soldiers, is the question of human suffering. As with the discourse about road transport, the safety of people is not a high priority. Ordinary folk, women particularly, go on protesting, unheard, against attitudes which seem official and statistical only. Recently BBC television presented a programme called *The Bull's-Eye War* about the accuracy and knock-out quality of modern weapons of mass destruction. The presentation of modern war was to some extent like that of a game. To be fair to the BBC, the *Radio Times* carried three lead letters on the topic a fortnight later, all three highly critical of the programme. It was pointed out that human values and human suffering were being played down in favour of a purely technical approach to a hypothetical East–West military conflict. Readers expressed disgust and despair, and implied that they detected a kind of obscenity or pornography in certain attitudes expressed. Perhaps the most hopeful aspect of these letters was the identification of pornography with violence, not merely with sex, as is usual.

Military pornography. Somehow we have got to make people see that the central pornography of today is the pornography of impersonal and insensitive violence. The Churches and the education service, mindlessly lost in centuries-old suspicion of sexuality, have just not woken up to this as yet, and don't want the 'purity' of their ideas soiled by contact with the practical realities and the practical action which movements against war would make necessary. For all the misery which it justifies, the independent state, or superstate bloc, gets away, without condemnation, not just with murder, but, potentially, with a million murders. The state cannot be tried and cannot be sentenced—nor can it be disgraced and driven from its job.

In fact the whole evil structure of independent nationhood, in the past the source of so much poetry and piety, is, in the quite new, modern world, upheld by industrial leaders who make money out of armaments, and would not be able to do so under a world police force so effectively and so frequently; and by soldier-statesmen who need to use chaos between nations as avenues for their own lusts for power. The former educational structure, especially that in public schools, supports the whole dreary international scene with military training, very formal discipline, and above all by the absence of empathetic education. And this brings us to the education of those who control the armies, the bombs.

Many diplomats have had a very formal education. At school they have faced much austerity, and at university severe intellectual rigour. Emotional response and empathy, personal relationship, relaxation, will have been typical of the kind of things they have been taught to think less worthy than toughness, manipulation of people and events, and the arduous nature of achievement. These traditional conditions do not encourage a steady and sensitive view of man's total destiny on this pathetic and tragic blob of Earth. The public schools must take the lion's share of the blame, for they have been the slowest to acknowledge new types of experience leading to a balanced tension between intellectual and emotional development.

Most diplomats are highly experienced, highly-skilled men and women, working arduously with relatively little public recognition—that much must be said. It must also be said that the world's Foreign Offices are badly in need of a few new ideas. Thank God there are some men and women of vision in these places, but the work of others is marked by a lack of creativity, an emotional and spiritual failure to care for the world as a whole. Yet nowhere in the political field do we so desperately need as here those precious gifts of imagination which a formal education withers in the bud. Our diplomats need, desperately, to imagine and plan for new things, if we are all to be saved. This means ceasing to rely on old-fashioned pacts and treaties and secret agreements entirely; it needs feeling, creativity and imagination; it needs new structures. It means not just leaving a nasty international situation in its traditional unsatisfactory mess until a crisis supervenes, and then desperately trying to patch it up. It means removing the causes of war; it means the rule of law, of a world police; it means willingness, and ability, to change old ideas about nationhood and about sovereignty.

Our job in education—nobody else will do it—is to educate people to demand better statesmanship, and to help to produce statesmen with more love in their hearts, and with the flexibility and imagination which go with love. Like those civil servants who drive people off the rails on to our dangerous roads because they have not had the imagination to bother enough about horrific road casualties; like the civil servants who have approved intensive farming without feeling for the millions of suffering animals; so our under-imaginative diplomats will not take into their hearts and minds the hideous reality of what may happen to the world if we cling to old ideas.

How excellent it would be to involve Churches, schools and higher education in this work of eliminating world violence. Just now we all seem apathetic. It was said recently, in connection with disturbing revelations of brutal corporal punishment in Scottish primary schools, that there had not been a squeak of protest from any Church people in Scotland, while the education service itself was evasive. About the horrors of war too, and the absurdity of our international anarchy, there is the same disturbing silence, broken only by lonely and intermittent voices, chiefly from the Quakers and the nonconformist Churches. Yet we need a national movement in favour of goodness and peace; an alert electorate whose reaction to the war-planes which tear daily across our skies will be to see them as an appalling waste, a sign of the failure of diplomats whom we have charged not only with the preservation of peace but also with the making of peace.

In our schools we must devise a curriculum which asks questions about international society and about ways of peacefully and democratically securing a peaceful world order. We must provide a climate where money and competition are played down in favour of love, peace and a universal empathy which moves across frontiers. The arts will have to be brought into full scope in the development of this sense of kinship with life all over the globe, helping us to bring forth people who do not want to defoliate other people's land and kill people of a different colour on a different side of the globe. Vague goodwill is no longer enough: the international

69

meetings of students, and the international work-camps, have been good, but not enough: we have to organize, not for communism, not for capitalism, or for any limiting ideology, but for peace.

Says Emery Reves:

> We must get this problem discussed in groups, meetings and on platforms. Universalism and the imperative need for universal law must resound in all houses of God. The universal outlook of political and social matters must be taught in all schools. We should elect nobody to public office who has not pledged himself in advance to work whole-heartedly to prevent the next war by the establishment of peace through law and government. . . . In every field of human effort we aim at perfection. . . . Yet, when we are faced with the problem of peace, perfection becomes a smear word.[3]

---

[3] Emery Reves, *The Anatomy of Peace,* Penguin 1947

CHAPTER 7

Bogus Social Discipline

We are presented with a world of disorder: the key-word of traditional education has always been discipline. The word even survives, a little quaintly, as a description of areas of study within a university. It has a nicely portentous ring. Education, it appears, is essentially to do with order. To be educated, people have to exercise arduous control over subject-matter and over themselves. Educational manuals with many chapters survive from past generations to instruct people about moral training and strict discipline.

The idea of control is central—and somewhere, behind all the talk, lies the brave and somewhat naïve idea that if we all became controlled and somehow 'pure' we should make the whole world decent and pure too. This is very like the optimistic belief of evangelists and their followers that if we all became saved the world would become perfect. Unfortunately, just as traditional evangelism leaves out so much when it tries to define impurity, so education also seems to latch on to the wrong things, the unimportant things. The result in both cases is disconnection between the world inside and outside; a cocooned existence.

In the world 'outside', for example, the media are wildly and anarchically free, to pursue us, to lie to us, to persuade us to buy all sorts of stupid and hurtful things, and to present violence *ad lib*. Anarchy also reigns with regard to international affairs, and here we seem to be preserved from destruction only by lucky breaks. Moral anarchy reigns, more or less unquestioned, in the field of economics. Even in our 'decent' country we are still learning that many of our dividends come from sweated labour abroad, though we believed that we had done with the bad old days; while at home the union bosses on the one hand and the more selfishly profiteering leaders of industry on the other seem to equal one another in their zeal for bringing the country to its knees. Meanwhile the speculator, the builder, the roadmaker, the

71

developer, are slowly and steadily spoiling the face of the land, and are only fitfully and inadequately checked by weakish legislation. Moral anarchy rather than the rule of law is characteristic of much government business. It is slowly becoming apparent that even in the better democracies like ours there are, amongst the many good and honest men in government service, con men, quislings, put in, at every level from parish councils, through district councils, right up to the ministries and the House of Commons, to support special private groups. Again, fitful attempts at control, increasingly argued for, are largely futile. It is becoming commonplace here, as it has often been abroad, to talk about 'fiddles'. Too much public business is being settled over good wine in expensive clubs, and all this is beyond adequate control, and many good men just will not serve in local or national government because of the chicanery which everybody knows about. We don't talk about this in schools.

As a nation we cannot control the endless and heartless cruelty to animals, or to children, or to the neglected handicapped people who lack adequate medical and pastoral help. We cannot control the wholesale abuse of social priorities, when hospitals and schools and social services languish for lack of aid, while offices and multi-storey car parks and elaborate road-works and elaborate armaments and projects like Concorde take up our money, taxed from us and used against us. In my own college one over-worked secretary is all we can afford to service three large departments, yet on my way into town I see the bulldozers working on the ring road all through weekends at double pay, providing jobs, at £50–£70–£100 per week. Even our police force, the symbol of public order, a wonderful historic development, is in some cases 25 per cent short of adequate personnel, though labourers and mechanics paid at fantastic rates are readily found for other projects. Ordinary people are progressively being denied basic freedoms in their choice of goods, the manner in which they move, and the space available around them. The increasing uniformity of shopping, as the huge super-stores move forward, is diminishing choice as much as it diminishes the personal touch: with the closure of railways people have less and less choice as to how they move about the face of the Earth: even space is pre-empted for them by developers:

A tree-planting scheme was promised but when it came to it the County Council said the spaces the builder had left were too near the road. I think there should be play areas within the estate where the children can meet socially . . . these things have to be fought for. They are not planned. . . . It is the builders who do the designing, not architects.[1]

And as if all this were not enough, we have left too much freedom in the hands of a trivializing bureaucracy in so many walks of life, manipulating people, usually beyond any legal or parliamentary control. These colourless Establishment figures, fundamentally clean and 'decent', snooping, puppeteering, wearing people out with forms and pointless meetings and procedures, are a unique product of our century. They exist in almost all countries and almost all areas of human activity, including education. Colin Morris has written magnificently about them:

Their values are so inane that they are no more an effective check upon the fantastic power at their disposal than a wrapping of Christmas paper around an elephant. They talk; their mouths open and sentences tumble out that serve only to punctuate the silence. By their bumbling, they have so trivialized honest emotion that words like sacrifice, love and duty have to be scrubbed with disinfectant before they can be spoken without a sneer. . . .

They destroy their detractors by clasping them fondly to their bosoms and asphyxiating them. They are so decadent as to make ancient Byzantium seem like the New Jerusalem, and yet so decent that even when they are clubbing you to death you feel impelled to apologize for spilling blood on their carpet.[2]

'The fantastic power at their disposal.' Most of the worst things in our society are not only beyond the control of ordinary folk but are not even recognized, not even talked about; huge firms proliferate and take over the Earth without any consultation with anyone at all.

Our reaction in educational circles is farcical. When wildly lashing about looking for a theory of discipline we are careful to make it irrelevant. At its imbecile extremes it produces head teachers who become hysterical because a boy's or girl's

[1] Rachel Semlyen and Greta Barnes, 'Farewell to the "Old-Fashioned" Yorkshire Village?', *Yorkshire Ridings Magazine,* June 1975
[2] Colin Morris, *Unyoung, Uncoloured, Unpoor,* Epworth Press 1969, pp. 80—1

hair is too long, or because a boy and a girl are seen kissing on the way home from school, or because somebody's school uniform is not quite right; yet if one thing emerges from the immoral 'decency' of all the nasty non-sexual things that go on in the world at large it is that old notions of 'purity' are now inadequate, and this is to say nothing more than to ask that we go back to the words of Jesus, who said that purity lay in the motives of the heart, not in technicalities.

We are a mad nation. Which is worse, a boy/girl passion at school, or the annual loss of 66,000 acres of pure farmland in this country each year: that is, 100 square miles, or the loss of a county the size of Berkshire every five years? Or the plan, still extant, to blast a motorway through the heart of some of the best countryside between two major cities along the line of a perfectly good and much safer railway?—and this at a time when Britain needs to move towards a self-supporting situation, using its farmland with greater wisdom and intelligence! It is big business which needs disciplining. Some of the worst schemes for despoiling the land are only held back by the current recession and by the shortage of the one thing which is driving us all mad—money. The ways of undisciplined money are not only unwise but also unimaginative and monotonous. So some of our road schemes are parallelled on a much vaster scale by the scheme to drive a huge motorway through that great oxygen-factory of our world, the Amazon jungle. 'Every time you cut down a tree, you destroy a world.' The realities of the social and ecological damage, and of the natural and usable river waterway already existing, are not observed. Love is sometimes said to be blind, but money is the truly sightless medium.

When we are not getting steamed up about sexual purity we are wildly insisting on the control of hard work, asking pupils to sacrifice more and more time and all the distractions of the flesh. Keep your head down and don't think of anything else! All personal relations are jealously watched: pupil to pupil: pupil to teacher. But for the rest, for the national and international and commercial scene outside, well, we just ignore it. No wonder that our pupils grow up with warped notions of discipline and what it means. In education's tacit support for the corruption outside its locked doors it is, again, very like evangelistic movements. The purity/sex syndrome forms a

74

very useful smoke-screen which operates to prevent people from seeing the sheer lack of control, the raging, unchecked, legal, acceptable, bloody awful selfishness outside.

Our notions of discipline and control need a one hundred and eighty degrees turn. We need to teach ourselves to fear not the kiss, the personal relation, the relaxation, the physical pleasure, the penis, but all the raging, uncontrolled pseudo-phalluses—the car with the aggressive driver, the cigarette, the missile, the cold pen of the bureaucrat. We need to free people, but establish control over machines, including human machines. These suggestions do not imply any wild emotional or sexual free-for-all. The need is rather to help people towards tender and sensitive and inner forms of discipline based on concern for others they know, and for the human race generally, and there must be new and saner checks almost certainly on the number of children we can have. Sexual hygiene and contraception need new emphasis, backed up with a climate of responsible freedom, massive support for counselling services, and the sensitivity provided by the proper teaching of the arts as well as by the sciences. But we really must stop being afraid of love. Love is a good thing, desire is a good thing; love and desire and pleasure, not competition and violence, cross frontiers and bind together the human family. The best way of sending men out to do battle with the giants of the world outside, is to send them out from a free and happy family which has found life happy enough and fulfilling enough to be worth preserving.

At present machines and money and administrators are running amok, while people, in spite of surface appearances of permissiveness, are over-controlled. We need to put machines, quite literally as well as metaphorically, back on the rails; and take people off.

CHAPTER 8

The Paradox We Do Not Face

Isn't life a terrible thing—thank God.
DYLAN THOMAS
Under Milk Wood

One of the odd assumptions beneath traditional educational orthodoxy is that all is well. With a kind of obscene optimism, bred out of indifference to suffering 'outside', we believe that the present school system, the present higher education system, the present examination system, are good—given perhaps a few technical changes here and there: that jobs will be waiting at the end of courses, that these jobs will be worth while, and that happiness will arrive in due course. Keep your heads down! It's a sensible, well-groomed world. It is the world, *par excellence,* of the traditional grammar school and public school. Its values are static.

But if we take a reformist view like that described in the chapter above, the world looks different. A reformist view might make us happier and more caring in the present, our sole possession, but it would do so partly to prepare us for battle with the darkness 'outside'! Existing values would be questioned, and our view of the life to which education is a response would be basically a tragic one—in so far as a tragic view implies constructive discontent and compassion and amelioration, nor merely gloom. It might even imply a new kind of cheerfulness.

In the past the only hint of tragedy in education has been the heroic invocation to fight and die in order to defeat one's country's enemies. But now the enemies are everywhere, without and within, and in our hearts. (George Bernard Shaw spent his life trying to teach us this.)

The optimist/pessimist paradox, the knot entwined at the heart of life, the recognition that life is marvellous and at the same time quite dreadful, is something we barely acknowledge in education, unless perhaps we are dealing with some work of art which forces it upon us. Or perhaps the sensitive teaching of Religious Knowledge reveals to us its presence in the life of Christ. In fact it is everywhere. On the walls of my tutorial room are two pictures. One is the *Fighting Téméraire,* Turner's famous and tragic portrait, ironic in title and execution, of the fine ship going to her last berth to be broken up. With its lurid sunset glow, it almost certainly had autobiographical overtones for Turner himself. My other picture is of a massive and powerful steam locomotive, *The Evening Star,* in all its pristine glamour and colour. Both pictures say something true about life—life is great, life is gloomy, life is romantic and full of verve, life is ironic and pathetic; and life ends. We don't educate for the end, for death. We should value the present more if we did.

Man is the measure of all things, says one picture. Man is a tragic failure, says the other. Life is abundantly worth living: life is also wasteful, silly and sad. This steady ambivalence, once acknowledged, puts all that we do into tragic perspective. It makes much over-serious committee work look like the posturings of madmen. This is the type of experience, the coming face-to-face with futility and alienation, which has been the germ of so much existential writing—which lies behind Paul Tillich's insistence that until we realize our helplessness and isolation, and can accept our plight, we cannot find a form of healing and a kind of relationship with others which is based on reality.

Indeed, though we assume that we are educating for optimism and sanity, are we, in a practical sense, sane at all? We say that we love peace, yet so weak is our control over death-dealing things that the windows of our toy-shops are full of tanks and machine guns. Of the *Radio Times* letter-writers about *The Bull's-Eye War*, mentioned earlier, all three appeared to doubt the basic sanity of our species. Surely many of us must feel this. The pathetic pretence that re-armament will always make 'the others' stop re-arming is such a ridiculous non-starter that one doubts the basic mental balance of those who maintain it. In fact the manic spiral of fear and tension always goes on. Great Powers behave like stupid children, pretending that national prestige, and abstractions like 'democracy', 'the Western way of life', 'the class struggle', 'the will of the proletariat', are worth the blowing-up of the world. A normal child of eight could teach them otherwise; needing life, love and hope, he would dismiss this as pie in the sky.

We say we wish to preserve life and morality, but so dense are we that legalism is always overpowering practical sense. So—we make a tremendous fuss about the termination of an early pregnancy through abortion, but don't get half so steamed up about the daily agonies undergone by real, living, fully-developed children because of traffic accidents, or parental neglect, or unnecessary bereavement, or whatever: we prefer to defend an unformed thing in preference to a terrified, screaming, bereaved, wounded or lonely child, which is where the need for love really comes in. We do almost nothing to prevent a war in which millions of children would go through hell—many anti-abortionists seem unaware of these larger issues. We live in a world where a doctor or a teacher may be driven from his job because he has fallen sincerely in love with a patient or a pupil; where a lorry-driver who has knocked down and mortally injured a middle-aged cyclist (against whom no negligence is proved, who lingers desperately in hospital for four days before dying) is fined £25; where a man found once only in possession of cannabis is fined £75, although cannabis has not yet been proved to kill anybody (in America he might have been jailed for ten years or even executed); where anyone, including high government officials in the education service, and headmasters, may openly buy and smoke cigarettes, although they kill 50,000 people each year in Britain alone. In the face of such absurdity, such evidence of the effect of money on the process of law, one feels that ironic amusement, even if that be bitter, is inadequate as a response; only a kind of despairing contempt for such a world seems adequate.

Our sexual *mores* are often ridiculous. Most people know that farmyard-type promiscuity does not produce true happiness, but orthodox moralists are wrong when they pretend that orthodox marriage and pre-marriage is the near-to-perfect answer, whereas these are in fact imperfect traditions which have great capacity for isolating people as well as for helping and releasing them. Crude immorality is bad, but orthodox morality often intensifies feelings of failure and guilt. There is no perfect answer to the enigma of relationships in a most imperfect world. As one of my most perceptive students says, with an eye upon her own scientific discipline, 'Relations with other people are the only things which have not advanced over the years.' Man has been given a terribly sticky wicket to bat on in all matters relating to sex and childbirth—trouble stares him in the face at every turn, and to act freely yet responsibly is supremely difficult. Yet without freedom he is a zombie and without responsibility he is a devil. People need immense sympathy in the matter of personal relations: less censure, more help. Hundreds of marriages are in jeopardy not because of 'sin', but because one or both partners lack skill, or warmth, or both in the art of love, and they are victims of earlier denial of love. Hosts of people need sympathetic counselling. But we can't find money for counselling: we throw the world's money down the two bottomless pits of re-armament and economic competition.

Education for reality must include the recognition that Man is both victim and tyrant. He is not responsible for a cruel universe in which he can scarcely live, breathe, wear clothes and shoes, even work, without killing or oppressing other living things: even vegetable life, some people now believe, 'feels' pain when it is cut down. At the same time, though insensitive to the suffering he causes, man suffers a great deal himself—his life is often sad, sometimes agonizing. Yet he completes the dark scene by oppressing his fellows and exploiting the Earth. He is often not just lower than the angels but lower than the animals. How can the innocent and suffering whale, the badger with his cleanly habits and adorable family play, compare with ruthless businessmen scorching up the motorways, with the mindless young vandals who wreck and riot in our cities, or the men and women in war factories making jellied petrol? To make the comparison is an insult to the badger, the whale. We stink. We cannot begin a proper theory of education until we know that we stink.

And all the time we tell lies. Our politicians tell lies. Our advertisements tell lies. We are called upon not to bear false witness. The old-fashioned, independent nation-states and super-states make extravagant claims about their superiority to other countries which are false but also vulgar: no gentleman would thus shout his own virtues from the house-tops: and this arrogance is a danger to us all.

We train people not to see all this. Yet one can see the point of Hardy's view, put forward pre-eminently in that seminal book, *The Return of the Native,* that our duty is not to try to advance in life with renown but to contract out of it without shame. And how alien that is to all our educational theories as we have them at present.

One realizes with renewed force the social effect of all the examination grind and the irrelevant fact-grubbing. Keep your heads down! Don't look up, or you might realize the state of things and do something about it—you might even cry!

And yet! To see life merely as it if were hell, a twentieth-century hell, is surely not right. A student of mine, a realist with her feet on the ground, writes of her pleasure, in a dark time, in the going home to a well-loved family at the weekend, of a simple evening out with her boy-friend. Still, love abounds. The country, still fighting back the developers, is still beautiful. Children, movingly, if they have been brought up lovingly, assume that life is great, and prepare to laugh their way through it with a wisdom as old as the hills. In dark times personal relations can still retain—perhaps more significantly because the skies are dark—that numinous quality which can turn classes into groups and meetings into encounters and enable us to look honestly into one another's eyes. To the person who is trying to see life steadily and see it whole, life is no longer the flat wash of pseudo-optimistic grabbing and mugging-up and competing which education would have us capitulate to. Nor is it purely a hell (a horror generally ignored by education). It is light and dark, with the light as real as the dark. In a tragic world, the world of Hiroshima and Vietnam, of beaten horses and broken-hearted kids, the total view also helps us to acknowledge the presence of beauty, joy and laughter—that kind of assertion of life which breaks through the darkness of Beethoven's last quartets to give us love, and sometimes, sheer lightness of heart. The truly educated man has to be Janus-like—he sees both heaven and hell. The final tragedy of modern education, the work of a few brave experimenters apart, is that it is blind in both pairs of eyes. It sees neither the darkness which it should help people to lighten, nor the love and the beauty of life which is ultimately the only reason for worthwhile living. It is totally, and it sometimes seems irremediably, blind.

Deceiving People

We can find a way back towards an existential, a real theory of education which seeks to help, if we admit the disorder and the madness as well as the order, if we stop trying to find patterns which aren't there. We have to educate for disorder, for alienation; for man's sin; for man's madness; not for a cocooned middle-class existence. Says John Wilson:

> The human situation is tragic . . . the 'normal' or 'natural' condition of man is profoundly unsatisfactory. On this view man is radically unlike other animals: he is a freak, something thrown up by nature without proper provision for his happiness, a permanently discontented animal. There will be plenty of things in everyone's mind, which went wrong in his childhood, which he has to be educated out of. If we want to improve the human condition, we must regard the process not as one of building on to an already sound structure, but as one of recouping what has been lost: of enlarging and thereby strengthening the consciousness, of recovering something of the strength and energy of our desires, of freeing them from guilt and fear which blended with them almost at their very inception.[1]

We need an education with its eyes open. We need a radical philosophy to re-shape our aims in favour of a life-style suited to the real world. It has to be a life-style to help people. At present a few people in the churches, and a few young folk experimenting with new forms of philanthropy, are almost alone in this. It is time that we in education helped them.

[1] John Wilson, *Logic and Sexual Morality,* Penguin 1965, ix, pp. 236–7

The great English Universities, under whose direct authority school-children are examined in plays of Shakespeare, to the certain destruction of their enjoyment, should be prosecuted for soul murder.

A. N. WHITEHEAD
Aims in Education

New Members Welcome

Pull the blinds
    on your emotions
Switch off your face.
Put your love into neutral
This way to the human race.

SPIKE MILLIGAN
Small Dreams of a Scorpion

PART TWO

Hurting People

CHAPTER 9

Getting People Worried (1)

Education reflects the world it exists to serve. I sometimes go out with my students to look at people in the streets, in shops, in cafés, and ask them to come back to talk, write, draw, paint. They usually conclude that they have seen a lot of strained, unhappy, defensive people.

It would be foolish to suggest that education has caused all their troubles, but it is to many people a potent source of worry, tension and fear, some of which persist for years after formal education is finished. Education, as well as blinding people to many of life's greatest realities and greatest needs, is a major direct contributory factor in the world's unhappiness, especially with regard to the more intelligent pupils.

There are the extreme examples. The following are both from young teachers I know, the first from a young woman working with delicate children:

> One of my pupils, a clever boy in his fourth year, died the day the results came out. He had returned home after the exams after eighteen months of perfect health with us, but when subjected to his parents' semi-cruelty became so depressed that when he went into *status/asthmaticus* he was unable to fight it. I received one letter from him telling me how miserable he was at home, then nothing. He had the type of parents who insisted on work, work, work. Leisure was not to be tolerated. I used to fight them when they visited him, telling them he *would* do well. He and I resolved to show them, and we both worked hard. We had lots of fun, and giggled constantly as we sorted out the Maths problems. Anyway, he achieved two Grade 1, one Grade 2 and one Grade 3. I was so thrilled. Then he died.

—and one from the now largely-discredited 'eleven-plus' examination—the announcement of 'results':

The Head walked into the classroom holding the results, but then indulged in a long conversation with the form-master. This built up tension and ensured emotions would be high when the results were given. The Headmaster then announced the results very slowly, telling each child to stand as his name was called. Finally, the list was complete. We, the successful, stood; they, the failures, sat. They sat first in silence, hoping for more names, and then remembered the prizes offered by their teachers and parents and realized their humiliation. Many of the girls and some of the boys wept.

On that day, many seeds of snobbishness on the one hand, and envy, inferiority and hatred on the other, must have taken root.

These are just some of the blatant horrors. What are the routine facts?

1. Resentment

Most pupils dislike the education they receive. It is difficult to quote figures, since no one seems to do much research in this field, though many much more trivial issues are researched thoroughly. It is confirmed by hundreds of conversations. It is not true of the good primary school, the most hopeful area of education, and not true of the student who fits well into higher education and follows his real interests within a humane faculty. It is true of the bad primary school, of the higher education student who can't find the course to suit him or is inhumanely handled or should't be in higher education at all. It is abundantly true of many secondary schools, and almost universally true of pupils unwillingly kept at school because of the raising of the school-leaving age.

What are the consequences? Does all this hurt people? If we suppress the puritan mental cliché about the virtues of being bored and fed up and undergoing discipline for its own sake—yes. Miserable experiences without obvious purpose breed rebellion and resentment. Unhappiness at school is associated with vandalism and lack of respect for authority, ways of getting back at adults for all the frustration.

The roots of goodness lie in loving relationships within family life. Schools and colleges with warm relationships, including within their climate the fun and humanity which are the food of goodness and love, confirm growth in order and goodness. Educational institutions which run counter to the best values of family life are undoing the work of good parents, and contributing not only to unhappiness but also to the violence of a disordered and resentful society. Parents who have treated their own children with the love and respect due to them as growing young people, often seem prepared to hand their children over to other people who will treat the same children as ignorant, stupid and simply as objects. This is very surprising; and I think it can only be explained in that again we are being brain-washed into doing this because it is customary.

2. Personal tension

For the less conscientious pupils the nastiness of so much education is relieved by *graffiti* in the lavatories and by general vandalism, and later by over-blatant assertion of individual freedom at society's expense. Whether you terrorize the neighbourhood on your heavy motor-bike, or rape a district as a property-developer, or rape a country by bombing and invading it, you may well be getting back at society for the contradictions and denials of your childhood when love was first expressed or at any rate needed and then denied. Plenty of biographical material about 'great' and powerful men confirms this sort of diagnosis.

For the conscientious and sensitive pupil who goes up and up the school and college ladder the effect may be markedly different. Many pupils can put down life-long tension habits, vague continuous worry, inability to enjoy books, general feelings of guilt when they try to relax, to the years of unremitting struggle to improve standards and pass examinations. Factors worth thinking about in this connection include homework, and the function of tension-relievers.

It is odd that while tough men in the trade unions fight for increasingly shorter hours with long, paid holidays, society is content to make its brighter children work as if they were galley-slaves without pay and without question.

Two children interviewed, one boy and one girl, were over-anxious about their G.C.E. 'O' level examinations, and spent every evening at lesson preparation and revision. They were encouraged in this attitude by their parents, and the girl accepted her restricted existence without question. The boy, intelligent and a lively conversationalist, was more resentful of his narrow life and made one striking statement: 'I work more hours than the children in the Industrial Revolution, I long for a new Shaftesbury to come to our rescue.'[1]

The homework, as many teachers when pressed will admit, is often only necessary because of bad teaching and bad timetabling at school, and because the syllabuses encouraged by the examining boards are overcrowded. 'Squeeze them till the pips squeak', is the belief of many educators; and how barbaric is this mental cruelty! The subjects at 'O' level have to be collected, as if they were conkers, in large quantities—why? There seems no justification in a civilized society for expecting young people to work, in many cases, from breakfast until bed-time while adults work, in many cases, for much shorter hours, or to accept without question the enormous social restrictions and the consequent loss of growth in personal maturation which these long hours entail. We are brutes to our most able kids.

Many parents are not aware of other hidden penalties. If the parents of college and university students knew the truth—about the results of depression and tension: about anti-depressants, tranquillizers and other props, there would be a public outcry. Every Dean of faculty and every university medical officer knows that many students, especially women, are only able to work in the months immediately preceeding their final examinations if prescribed vallium, librium, or a similar drug. Overworked doctors are compelled to prescribe these. What else can they do?—it is the educational system which is wrong. Moreover the incidence of hard drug-taking and of heavy drinking is certainly accentuated by educational stress. So is the traffic in soft drugs (cannabis) which in the view of Dr Benjamin Spock[2] is less harmful than the traffic in tobacco. Every students' union has its cigarette-machine. The cigarette is the most common way of finding strength to get on with an over-load of tedious work. Deaths from lung cancer and other diseases caused by the smoking habit are now, in

[1] Williams, K., and Miller, W., 'The Lonely Children', *New Education,* November 1966, p. 12

[2] See Benjamin Spock, *Bringing Up Children In A Difficult Time,* Bodley Head 1974, xxviii, xxix

England and Wales, four times greater even than the road fatality figures. Hundreds of thousands of students are hooked on the cigarette habit for life, to die miserably and earlier than they need, or at best to effect a permanent scar upon their health, because of smoking caused by stress while they are students.

3. Boredom
A young lady in the sixth form writes:

> I am now prepared to go to either Exeter or Manchester University if I can manage to gain high enough 'A' level passes in the summer. We have already started revising and doing past papers at school so the next six months will be rather tedious.

—and a young man—

> When I was a student, I hated Shakespeare and almost anything else before entering the sixth form, when we were given more freedom to choose what interested us, to say what we ourselves thought, and had more time to sort out our ideas. This lasted until our thoughts had to be funnelled down the straight and narrow path of 'A' level exams.

The late teens make up some of the most precious and receptive years of life, when the full tonal quality of existence explodes upon the eager mind. It is sad to think of so many young people condemned to plain boredom at this time. They miss hours needful for enjoying earth and air and the life of plants and animals, and for extending their own personal relationships; they plod on even during the long summer days, dredging up innumerable boring facts, employing only one facet of the mind, while the precious emotions and the intuitive side of life lie almost dead. One wonders what the full cost is, in terms of personal maturation, for some of these pupils.

4. Competition
A traditional argument in favour of the nastiness of education runs like this—By its toughness and nastiness it prepares pupils well for a nasty, tough world. The world certainly is tough and nasty, and some degree of grit is needed for survival. What is overlooked in this context is the hopeful fact

that, aggressive though man may be, he competes as eagerly with abstract problems and impersonal forces as with his fellows. He also competes well with his own second best. Internecine competition, encouraged in education, as in national rivalries and in commerce, is not necessary for the fulfilment of man's thrusting desire to conquer. The Americans and Russians, when deflected from the desire to crush each other as persons and nations, are happy to compete together against the problem of the conquest of space. The stressful competitiveness of education is connected not only with appalling social snobbery but also with the big shop on the corner which forces the little man on the other corner (who has been there for years) out of business. It also—and this is a neglected aspect—by preparing people for a nasty, brutal world, confirms and sustains that nastiness, and inhibits change.

CHAPTER 10

Getting People Worried (2)—Examinations

Only a longer book can do justice to the hoary question of examinations and here it will be only touched upon. Even a university journal can say this:

> *The Assumption That Anxiety is Necessary*
> We stress the value of an examination as an initiation ceremony and in some ways enjoy its primitive ordeal character—while vigorously denying this. This would seem to be a hangover of puritan morality according to which little is worth having that has not been attained through hard work, suffering, self-renunciation and the constant threat of failure. One must give up present gratifications for the sake of future gains. This is known as 'character building', and whereas most universities, like most schools, would deny that this is part of their objectives, it is nevertheless a frequent argument when university life is discussed.
>   What is discussed less often, and then usually with a degree of good-natured contempt, are the suicidal depressions of students, the annual outbreaks of hysteric dyslexia, the little psychosomatic illnesses which appear at examination time. . . .[1]

In fact we have the odd suicide or two in British universities before examinations in most years: there are hundreds of breakdowns. Anyone who has worked in a university knows the figure of the friendly, pipe-smoking don who secretly loves to see his students sweat. Anyone who has invigilated at university examinations knows the nasty feeling of superior power and complacency, as he sits down on the platform in the seat of authority to read his *Guardian* while young people go through the ordeal beneath him.

The arguments in favour of formal examinations are well known. They are said to test character and mental stamina. They are said to be absolutely fair. They are said to reduce the

---

[1] Oppenheim, A. N., Jahoda, M., James, R. L., 'Assumptions Underlying the Use of University Examinations', *Universities Quarterly,* June 1967, pp. 348–9

risk of personal bias in marking. They are claimed to be less wearing upon students than continuous assessment. These arguments make up some of the central planks in the conservatives' platform.

That formal, ritualistic examinations can be cruel is also a well-worn argument, but it is not always appreciated that the sensitive and the creative feel the strain most, and only supporters of a very primitive and barbaric survival-of-the-fittest creed can choose to overlook this. The awesome artificiality of the whole examination procedure, when teachers and tutors, with whom pupils may normally be friendly, suddenly turn into jailers, afraid to speak: when the door opens at 9.30 and you have to stop at 12.30 and have to be escorted to the lavatory in case you cheat: the artificial struggle with the clock, and the feeling of guilt you have about all the people you are letting down if you don't do well: all this can be agony to the nervous, to the diffident, and to the creative person who just does not parcel off bits of work in forty-minute stretches to leave time for checking. As one of my students says, 'I am very slow with my handwriting. I find the more you know, the worse it gets'.

The conservatives' platform is wobbly in other respects. The desperately important determining examination fixed for a set time on a set day is a grossly unfair proceeding. To those who know some of the practicalities in the case, the claim that it is fair makes up one of the biggest jokes in the education business. What of the girl whose menstrual period, or acute pre-menstrual tension, coincides with the vital day, which has been casually chosen, often by a group of men? What of the student recently bereaved, or otherwise depressed? What about sudden local tensions? A young lady known to me had to reach school for a vital examination during a bus strike. After enduring the sight of several empty vehicles without staff to run them, she finally secured a lift, and arrived at school flustered and late. It is surely fairer to let people work at times when they are at their best. One suspects that what the defenders of formal examinations really believe in is not fairness but the Great God Luck.

Continuous assessment is not more demanding than the formal examination if it is worked under humane conditions. It causes trouble either when it is mixed with formal examining elsewhere in the same institution, or when it is carried through without a friendly and trusting relationship between students and staff.

That examinations test character and stamina is just another one of those arguments in favour of toughness, and to the prejudice of sensitivity and creativity, which make the world what it is. Toughness is tested, possibly over-tested, sufficiently elsewhere.

That examiners far away who do not know the pupils they examine are able to ensure impartiality is an argument inapplicable in any case to many school, college and university examinations, and true only in that faraway examiners are usually innocent of unconscious or deliberate bias for or against a student. This argument is offset by its failure to take into account mitigating circumstances known only to people on the spot which may affect a student's performance. It is further offset by variable examining standards. It is well known that examining boards differ in their standards and in the number of passes applicable to school exams bearing the same name, and that degree standards are also variable. A university may claim the right to set its own standards, and this is a jealously-guarded liberty, and rightly so; though the onlooker may still raise his eyebrows at extraordinary variations (for example in the case of the nationally-esteemed B.Ed. degree which varies wildly from university to university in the matter of class divisions awarded).

At the level of the school examining-boards, punctilious and conscientious efforts are made to pin down and eradicate marking variations. But anyone who has been involved in the pernickety marking of, for example, a minor and unimportant detail in the examining of a set book for an English Literature paper, will know that efforts like these are doomed to failure by any meaningful token. This is because, in the end, you can only force examiners to toe the line when everything boils down to tiny, boring facts, and the more you boil them down the more irrelevant they become. Creativity just isn't like this!

During a break in the writing of this chapter I talked by accident with a fourth-year student about to take degree examinations. He had just lost his girl-friend. He was low, though normally an able, and indeed quite a tough, character. He had suddenly become subject to fits of crying. After four years of hard full-time study in a very rigorous department he felt quite unable to do justice to the seven three-hour papers which the university had decreed to be, without any significant element of assessment, the measure of his work. Moreover he blamed fourth-year examination tension in part for the failure of his relationship.[2] Other students, in quantity, bear witness to this kind of happening. Not only do stimulants and drugs come increasingly into play at exam time, but relationships suffer as well, some irremediably: students living in halls of residences and college flats are subject to screaming fits, and break up friendships; long-standing boy-girl relationships fragment under the strain. It is a high price to pay.

Overseas there is sometimes more sensitivity to this problem than there is in Britain. Even the punctilious Germans are reacting:

As record numbers of West Germans have been taking examinations this summer, criticism of the present system of testing—and its effects on examinees—seems to have reached a new peak. Roughly two students out of three are apprehensive over forthcoming examinations, according to a survey conducted by the Psychosomatic clinic of the University of Giessen. But a high proportion experience an abnormal degree of fear.

A further investigation carried out by the clinic found that almost one student in five went to an advice centre for help either shortly before, or during, their examinations.

The reasons most frequently given to explain this anxiety were that they knew the examiners only slightly or not at all, and that they felt that their whole future depended on the results.

Herr Rolf Morgenstern of the Psychotherapeutic Advice Centre in Frankfurt distinguishes between students who prolong their studies for as long as possible, and those who give up before completing their courses.

The Frankfurt centre has simulated examinations and this technique has proved successful in relieving anxieties. Pressure to achieve good results also affects schoolchildren down to a primary level and can cause severe headaches, vomiting, asthma and circulatory malfunctions, according to hospital consultant Dr Johannes Meinhardt, spokesman for a study group set up by the German Teachers Association and the Association of German Doctors towards the end of May.

The group says factors include the closing down of small coun-

---

[2] This student failed to secure an honours degree.

try schools, parental pressure, the proliferation of different subjects taught by different teachers and the competition for university places.

Similar sentiments have been expressed somewhat more forcefully by Herr Wilhelm Ebert, president of the Bavarian Men and Women Teachers Association. At a recent conference in Bassau, he argued that schools were in danger of becoming anti-educational establishments because a child's main motivation was the fear of obtaining bad marks.[3]

Some formal testing, as a check, on occasion, is probably necessary in most subjects—though it is interesting that even medical schools—critically concerned with precise knowledge—are experimenting with assessment techniques. But to make or break students with three-hour papers is not only cruel but also silly. Examiners are never prepared to admit two possibilities. One is that they are unconsciously securing revenge upon the next generation for the miseries they endured years before under examination stress. The second is that there is often an automatic repression of knowledge after the event when that knowledge has been crammed up unwillingly and under artificial pressure, so that much is quickly forgotten. What a waste!

And how vulgarly do formal examination procedures pander to pedantry. 'We finished Christology last term', cries a theology student, aeons of time and energy away from the reality of the compassionate Christ. I have not yet forgotten the sense of shame I felt as an invigilator when, after overseeing a university examination in modern languages, I watched and listened as the near-hysterical, over-driven students left. 'No more French for the rest of my life, thank God!' said one—and this after four years on a government grant. And we call this, in our obscurantism, education! At a prize-giving, at a degree ceremony, the gowned folk sit on the platform, the organ plays, the parents clap. But if you know something of the other side of the story, if you know about the ill-temper, and the medical facts, and the black coffee and the fags, and the hatred for so much of it engendered in young minds, and if you know that so much will be quickly repressed and forgotten anyway, and that very little of what has gone on has any relation either to improving our world or to personal maturation, you don't feel so enthusiastic.

The lack of concern for what really goes on in young people's minds is the worst aspect of the whole affair. There is the easy use of fear, and the sheer lack of interest in what it has done to people, provided they get their certificates. Said the wise and compassionate Whitehead fifty years ago, 'Each school should grant its own leaving certificate, based on its own curriculum . . . with its approved curriculum based on its own needs and evolved by its own staff.'[4] Oppenheim, Jahoda and James suggest, concerning university examinations, that '. . . it might make more sense to pay particular attention to *entry* (selection) examinations instead of *exit* examinations; a student, once admitted, would be regarded as capable of benefiting from the course he has chosen and all that would be needed would be a certificate of attendance. It is also well known that the Civil Service and many professional organizations conduct their own entrance examinations. It would be interesting to find out to what extent universities live in their own private world in which examination results matter tremendously, and to what extent degree results make sense to people in the world outside.'[5] Whitehead takes us back to the family, the caring world which knows its own students and sets its own standards and does not want unnecessary suffering, and is not managed by a large body of people a long way off in a faculty committee or on an examining board in a distant city.

While we go on making the sensitive and the frightened suffer most because of examinations, playing meanwhile into the hands of aggressive and over-demanding parents by so doing, our education system is a hurting one. Formal examining is designed to secure the rejection, even if this be not deliberate, not only of those who are not clever and not conscientious, but also of those who are not tough, even though they may be desirable as human beings. To make this point is not to plead for students to have an easy time and little else. There are other, better ways of securing from them worth-while work.

[4] Whitehead, A. N., *Aims in Education*, vi
[5] Oppenheim, Jahoda and James, op. cit., p. 351

CHAPTER 11

Wasting People's Time: Desensitizing (2)

The Head of English in a large grammar school writes to me:

> The steam-roller of the school curriculum, stodgy, futile, compulsory rote-learning for that soul-destroying, anti-educational 'O' level English Literature examination; the existence of teachers who are more like drill-instructors than educators; hoary text-books and hoarier attitudes; above all, his own timidity and mental laziness: these are just a few of the problems which face an English teacher. Difficulties stemming from the pupil are, by comparison, trivial! It is almost as though our educational system had been devised to destroy a child's potential.

When I was at school I learned to make chlorine, and I had to learn the formula, which I still, uselessly, remember:

$$MnO_2 + 4HCl = MnCl_2 + 2H_2O + Cl_2$$

I was kept in at break to learn this, parrot-fashion. Of the principles and purpose behind Chemistry I remember nothing. Lessons in science were a debilitating grind, and though they were part of the ill-devised mechanism which got me to university, they gave me an unfortunate prejudice against science for years. As a specialist in literature I have never had to make chlorine, nor do I routinely make nitrous oxide, another experiment I was forced to learn word for word.

Time is precious: the present is holy ground, says Martin Buber; it is all we have. We hurt people if we take significance away from their time, which is itself the laboriously worked-for fruit of long gestation, birth and rearing. (Every person, as part of his or her education, should visit the labour ward of a maternity hospital, seeing things, hearing things, to see what life is all about, what it costs.) We are only justified in taking significance from the present if the sacrifice is for the sake of a higher significance to come. We waste pupils' time if we thrust useless material at them. We waste pupils' time if we set the needs of staff and their teaching habits above the needs of students, and we waste their time if we desensitize them to humane and artistic feeling. Here are some problems:

1. The over-loaded syllabus

The pride felt by parents and teachers about the seven, eight or nine 'O'-level passes is sometimes misplaced. Few young people can sustain a genuine and useful interest in such a rag-bag! An integrated approach to knowledge, and the necessary groundwork of general enquiry and enthusiasm, undertaken in the good primary school, is the first need of the child after infancy. After that, and much earlier than is now possible, students should be allowed *for assessment purposes* to specialize in the very small number of subjects which really interest them. The time thus saved would be better employed in general (non-examined) education of the type proposed in Part 3 below: the rhythm of effort and relaxation thus achieved would give variety and colour to the present monotony of school life. The notion that everyone needs to know a lot about everything is a hangover from the increasingly discredited notion of the pursuit of unrelated knowledge for its own sake, in the hope that some of it will 'come in handy'.

2. Conflicting claims of staff and students

Schools and colleges, like all institutions, have built-in resistance to human needs requiring change in structure. So have examining boards. Hence the conservatism which depresses us. 'Papers' are kept in being not because they serve any realistic human need but because someone *in situ* wants to examine them. To be fair, a few boards receptive to new schema are now prepared to drop some topics and initiate others. But often one wonders, as with all machines, precisely who is benefiting.

A similar situation arises in higher education where faculty boards and other bodies prescribing courses do so not because students are interested in them, but because Mr X or Dr Y wants to teach them. One might add that if Mr X or Dr Y wish to offer them as options no one should have cause for complaint. But such is academic megalomania that remote and peripheral subjects are often made compulsory, and so the personal fetishes of staff are used to make other people suffer.

Empire-building of this sort is as characteristic of arts courses as of science courses and also of post-graduate courses in education. The needs of staff are real ones, and indeed in terms of help for research, study leave, and so on we often treat them very badly. But in terms of matter to be taught, the needs of students should come first.

3. Destroying sensitivity

Students are now rejecting some university arts courses. Tom McGrath says, ' "I got a grant and went to university all set to do an honours degree in English and drama. But . . . I got so tied up with the practical side of the theatre that I became really cynical about academic attitudes. Who said that arts courses produce existential impotence?" ' So 'he took an ordinary degree instead and had a good time at Glasgow University while he did so'.[1] Many arts courses are not like this: in my own college we work with certain very humane university departments. But others produce psychological casualties in large numbers—people afraid to feel at all.

The sterile impact of wrongly-handled, wrongly-analytical arts courses is more damaging in schools, because so many more pupils are affected. I was talking once with a young man queueing outside the Shakespeare Memorial Theatre at Stratford-upon-Avon. He had, he confessed, loathed Shakespeare all through school, and only a chance meeting in later life with a friend who brought him to Stratford had helped to undo the anti-educational effect of his education.

The fact is that we spend a great deal of money—not enough, but quite a bit—on Arts Council projects to popularize drama, opera, ballet, poetry and the best of the cinema. Then, idiotically, we ruin the imaginative potential and feeling for art in the hearts of thousands of children by using the arts as exam-fodder. Here the great examining boards must take the lion's share of the blame. Says my secondary Head of English again, *vis-à-vis* the 'comprehension test' techniques we often use to hack literature to bits, 'We don't stop in the middle of a Chopin prelude to do five-finger exercises.' How right he is. In the teaching of literature our feeling for dead forms of analysis, and our dead worship of facts, diminish and sometimes entirely obliterate feeling and excitement. One of

[1] Cordelia Oliver, 'Eye-opener', *Guardian,* 10.5.75

the blackest spots in the whole of British education is the 'O'-level English Language paper, with its wretched little poems, and chunks of essays and novels, which children without any safe-guarding love of literature are forced to analyse and summarize. Music and the visual arts similarly suffer under premature and wrong-headed analysis. In fact the capacity for creative analysis is a late-developing one, the domain of the specialist. Once pupils have made up their minds as to their interests, they are ready to enter the stage of 'precision' without damage to their sensibility: but not before.

If comprehension-tests there must be, there is no need to prostitute literature to it at the non-specialist level. I have myself used a bus-timetable for a comprehension-test. However boring I was, at least I wasn't guilty of vandalism.

The artistic experience is a precious and fragile thing. Art is a reconciling force, giving us a sense of a community of man within the human family, his hopes, his loves, his hates, his visions. To turn it into exam-fodder for the collecting of quantities of certificates is a crime. This is to put the point strongly, but without apology. Anyone can see that the world is full of powerful men whose creativity has been maimed, humanity blunted, decision-taking made inhuman, because their capacity to feel the poetry of life has been maimed by the teaching they have received.

It is odd that no one bothers much about financing research into the effects of teaching on the appreciation of the arts and on emotional development generally. Possibly the omission is a political one. It should be remedied. The Department of Education and Science should move urgently to set up an appropriate enquiry. The investigating body should not be Establishment-centred. It should take evidence directly and honestly from the people who matter—the kids.

CHAPTER 12

Conclusions

Conclusions drawn less from formal research, notably scarce, than from the experience of working and talking with hundreds of children and students indicate: (1) In a world already marred by much stress and unhappiness, education produces more of both. It produces misery and it produces tears. It produces depression, and dependence on damaging stress-relievers; (2) The examination system is a major cause of stress and its 'fairness' is open to question; (3) Students are expected to expend much time unproductively. Basing further conclusions on the (admittedly) more controversial matter of Part 1, I would add that (4) Education provides young people with an incomplete and distorted view of the world. That view blocks off vast areas of tragic experience and stimulates intellectual growth at the expense of emotional growth; (5) In its facile optimism and opportunism education encourages a supine acceptance of things as they are. I would add, perhaps most controversially of all, that (6) The values which correlate with the chief means and aims of education are war values.

Who will deliver us from this dreadful machine we have created: this machine which is now ruling us?

The Unproductive Man is not a Christian . . .
Prayer is the Study of Art,
Praise is the Practise of Art.
Fasting &c all relate to Art.

WILLIAM BLAKE
from the *Laocoön Plate*

But vain the Sword and vain the Bow,
They never can work War's Overthrow.
The Hermit's Prayer and the Widow's tear
Alone can save the World from fear.

For a Tear is an Intellectual Thing,
And a Sigh is the Sword of an Angel King.
And the bitter cry of the Martyr's woe
Is an arrow from the Almighty's bow.

WILLIAM BLAKE
from *The Grey Monk* (Pickering Manuscript)

Men are admitted into Heaven not because they have *curbed* and
govern'd their Passions or have No Passions, but because they
Have Cultivated their Understandings.

WILLIAM BLAKE
from *The Last Judgment*

Helping People

CHAPTER 13

Celebration

It is odd that the simplest concept of helping people, one of the best things in the world, should seem unusual, even alien, in a book about education. I mean about helping people personally, not as part of the rat-race. Surely it is the most natural thing to talk about. As things are, to talk about it in an educational context is like using a muscle grown weak from under-use.

Life, tragic though it may be, has an ultimate hope, a grace about it. After accounts of the devious omissions of education, and its sins of commission, Part Three must be both cheerful and constructive. If we are to help people, the basic task is to help them to enjoy themselves (not the worst thing in the world, though too many people in education seem to think so). In a world of suffering and corruption, it is all the more important to celebrate the life and hope and love we have, the clearness, the honesty, the candid acts of loving.

In the college where I work student groups working closely with staff break out, so far as set courses will allow, into spontaneous folk festivals and drama festivals, into poetry-readings, music-making, and into displays of the visual arts, often at the end of a year or a term. They are not merely ways of escape, and not merely ways of showing that we are undefeated. They seem to say most convincingly of all that education is about pleasure, free creative experience, and community. One remarkable thing about such ventures is that though they often begin with appropriate frivolity, they often end in a natural and unforced seriousness. They produce responsible and satisfying break-throughs in student-to-student, year-to-year, and student-to-staff relationships. They invariably have a beneficial indirect effect on academic work, and not only because of the better relationships secured. For students who are intending to teach, they provide insights into methodology which students find as useful as their more formal method lectures and tutorials. These techniques are models for the kind of creativity we need more of everywhere in education—not merely as a way of providing showy material for Speech Day, or as a way of keeping students amused at the end of term.

The trouble is that education is hag-ridden with formally-educated administrators, head teachers, examiners, inspectors and assessors, staid people used to the humdrum world of committees, with no experience of letting their hair down. They don't value creative experience because they don't understand it, and they fall back on the plain diet of hard grind and 'standards'. Their narrowness seeks always to confine others. Somehow we have to find ways of restraining such people when, by means of a kind of intellectual fascism, they seek to restrict the lives of others.

Every educational institution should have a celebration element in its curriculum. If the curriculum includes tragedy, as it should, it must include celebration. The element need not go by that name; its basic component should be creativity and relaxation, peace, and pleasure.

In A. S. Neill's former school, Summerhill, pupils were permitted to go to lessons as and when they pleased, and allowed to absent themselves provided that they were doing no damage to themselves or to the school community. Neill's policy paid off in the long run, because in the end pupils arrived at lessons because they wished to be there. One cannot expect anything like such progressivism in our heavily-conservative state system. But one might hope for some measure of compromise—perhaps for multiple-choice activity designed to reduce the pupil's sense of regimentation and win his co-operation. But this does mean increased creativity, because people are then 'doing their own thing', and better-motivated learning ensues because pupils are enjoying it. All this means cutting down on the rag-bag of compulsory courses.[1]

Yet how much opposition there would be! I know of one entirely-optional, deeply-appreciated course in practical art which formed part of a university course. It was squeezed out

[1] See Chapter 20

102

from the syllabus because the over-intellectual people running the show could see no merit and no academic *éclat* in it. Their judgement was invalid, because they were judging the matter with only one part, and that the calculating part, of their minds. They could not see that students needed informal experiences—that this is part of education. Meanwhile other highly-specialized compulsory courses, some irrelevant to the needs of many of their students, were still being provided.

The word 'relaxation' is vital. Somehow we must help students to relax, to get away from the worry, to get off the excess alcohol and the cigarettes, and rest creatively so that they can work better. Relaxation, deep meditation, physical movement as therapy: things like these can lead us, for part of our education time, away from the over-stressed intellect towards wholeness of mind and body and a sense of the body's grandeur. Keats spoke of 'diligent indolence'. It is a largely unrecognized educational virtue.

Informal, creative work can advance the cause of peace. Heaven knows that peace needs profound international organization, but it is also true, as Tom Paxton says, that it should begin with each one of us, quite personally. Many of us are sick of our noisy cities, of the streets where you can't hear your own voice, the whole urban howl and roar which we have been brainwashed into accepting as civilized and normal. We are weary of the scream of jets in the skies as they prepare for war. To help people to be quiet, to see where they are going, is a neglected duty we owe to our pupils. There are strong grounds for suggesting that we should all be less war-like if we all engaged in some form of meditation each day. We should certainly be better off if we didn't have 'The News' with all its stressful and cruel undertones thrown at our heads every hour on the hour.

Creative, choice, celebration, relaxation, peace and pleasure. They are all unfashionable words in education. We are so used to the bloodless grind. That these words are unfashionable is further proof of the double blindness of education. But if life is seen as tragic, and therefore dynamic and in need of amelioration, then there is also, as Paul Tillich reminds us, 'a grace in life. Otherwise we could not live.' The fact that we want to change things proves that life is still worth living. Real celebration is celebration of growth and change and increased communication. Many teachers and lecturers have forgotten how to be really happy, how to relax—except through the power game, or by propping up the bar after work, or by organizing inane sherry parties. In all this there is little real joy, and certainly not much real communication. If, as I believe, education must wake us up to tragedy, it must also wake our pupils up to joy. Who will unbandage the eyes of education, those two sets of blind, Janus-like eyes?

CHAPTER 14

Towards a New Life-style: More Freedom

Changing the lay-out of the matter to be taught is not enough. Attitudes of both teachers and taught need changing, and though much work in sixth forms and in higher education is now highly informal, not least in England and in North America, in many cases we still think too rigidly of a class rather than of a group. Still too often, even in this country, and still more in Scotland and in Ireland and in many continental countries, learning and teaching are thought of as forms of indoctrination rather than as shared experiences. To say all this is not to deride the formal lecture, the formal demonstration—these are indispensable elements in education—but to draw attention to the rhythmic claims of formality and informality in teaching.

When we work in groups, rather than in classes, we have enough humility as teachers to be willing to believe that young people have something relevant to say to others and to ourselves, and that they may teach us valuable things. At least, we then know what they are thinking, their needs. There are many books about group experience—encounter groups, more or less radical; therapy groups in a medical setting; new attempts at communication in today's polite suburbs by means of house discussion groups. In the present context all I wish to do is to press the idea of group experience as a teaching model not necessarily confined to institutions explicitly concerned with education.

Groups, as distinct from meetings and committees, encourage sharing of experience, and throw emphasis upon people for their own sake rather than upon the systems and institutions which committees are invented to support. Groups break down, more or less, people's fears about loving and communicating. Because people find new inter-personal freedom, they begin to realize the supremacy of people over things. Because they talk about new things and reveal new anxieties they learn the values of intuition, laughter, instinct,

105

imaginative sympathy and mutual help, while still giving reason and calculation their proper due. Because they enjoy meeting people at a new informal level they become less interested in the customary glut of material possessions or in the lonely exercise of power. They also become more critical of a world which, they increasingly perceive, does not encourage communication of the type they are enjoying. In other words, groups help people to become persons rather than remain person-machines.

All this has unobtrusive but explosive implications for education. Consider, for example, the havoc wrought in life by externally proud and internally insecure figures who have been afraid to admit weakness. Many of the worst despots in history, and many of the worst teachers, have been like this. Adolf Hitler, and the Kaiser who precipitated the Great War are classic examples. Only informal education can prevent the emergence of these desolating iron men, where family life has denied them loving experience sufficient to give them natural confidence. Educated in formal classes and examined and tested by people who have pushed problems to them with cold fingers at the end of a long arm, the Kaiser Wilhelms of this world can cover up their inner unhappiness without fear of detection until such time as, in an effort to prove that they have no weakness, they take revenge on other people. It is horrific to reflect that many prominent figures in education are like this too.

The therapy of a good family-type group is such that, gradually, group members can bring the barriers down, admit their weakness, their fears and sorrows, find that these are shared with others, and begin to heal themselves. We have all been educated to be tough, but not educated to realize that our strength may be made perfect in weakness, that to be men also means humility and even, possibly, the bowing of our heads in sorrow. As Paul Tillich says, it is at the moment of complete desolation, when we admit to it, that we may find acceptance and love. How often, through the artificial conviviality of a non-communicating sherry party or something similar, has one suddenly seen the true shadows upon another's face and realized that the real need has been for the therapy of a good cry. The group can teach us our true dependence upon one another; how people need people.

106

In groups we can also find a new inner freedom. We appear to be living, and Tillich would have us accept our helplessness in having to live, within a partly-depraved world characterized by sealed and fated commercial systems which cannot be controlled, or so it sometimes seems: systems which are ruining the Earth and debasing Man and even seem to have infiltrated the legal system to produce a ludicrously inept system of penalties. Socially, too, many folk feel trapped, whether by class, moral attitudes, or the beliefs they have been told they must subscribe to under fear of penalty. In the freedom of inter-personal relations there is relief from the burden of fate: as Buber magnificently says, 'So long as the heaven of *Thou* is spread out over me, the winds of causality cower at my heels, and the whirlpool of fate stays its course.'[1] From that kind of freedom springs new hope of action on behalf of life, and this is likely to be of the kind mindful of people and considerate to people, not the wild, revolutionary plans of extremists in pursuit of some abstract cause. And even if nothing can be done in the world beyond the group, the new richness of inter-personal relations is endlessly available and people really know what each cares about, worries about.

Group experience can also make us less fearful of being loving. Mention has already been made of the chronic love-phobia characteristic of schools and of higher education. There really is no justification for herding students of adult age into segregated hostels against their wishes, because of our fears of men and women sleeping together. The only provisos to be made are that no one should disturb the peace of others, offend against public decency, or prevent those who wish to be segregated from being segregated. All the rest, in a world which needs more loving, and more responsible loving, is nonsense, and invasion of personal freedom. It would be far more to the moral point to ban cigarette-machines from colleges and universities. Incidentally, and with an eye purely upon academic work, many students would work better if they were untroubled by various sexual frustrations, and it has been known for years that many staff recognize this, and would like to see restrictions lifted, but have been afraid to express their views publicly. Proper student guidance and

[1] Martin Buber, *I and Thou*, T. & T. Clark, Edinburgh, 1970, p. 9

first-class counselling should prevent personal private free-dom from becoming anarchic freedom. In schools the issue is much more difficult, but we shan't be able to pretend for very much longer that sex should not bother older school-children or that it need not. It does. And that is not the pupil's fault. Many punishing and admonitory adults appear to have for-gotten that they once had explosive sexual instincts them-selves (unless they were abnormal and never had any). Some way will have to be found of accepting sexuality into the education of the under-eighteens—instead of treating it as devil no. 1—which is, as we have seen, a convenient way of ignoring all the other devils. We are handicapped all the time by centuries of faulty, over-serious, 'religious' teaching about sex.

The functions of sex as a kind of divine play, a much-needed relaxation for the psyche, as well as valuable inter-personal relating, have both been neglected. As Alex Comfort says, 'religion and psychiatry have unfortunately misread this play-function, as often as not, and set about converting what nature programmed as turn-ons and resources into hangups. Playfulness, like tenderness, is something our culture has undersold.'[2] Some parents and teachers have made sex dirty for so many children by loading it with guilt, and by implying that it is not the same as, or related in any way to, tenderness and any worth-while experience—by implying that it is merely getting away with something you shouldn't get away with: and can't unless you're cunning. Most significant and valid works of art shout 'Rubbish!' at us, of course, every time we imply this. But—'Only connect'. You only make physical feelings really find by accepting them and merging them in the minds of young people with feelings of tenderness and responsibility.

Part of the trouble is our morbid fear of touch. In normal converse it is traditional only to touch people by means of the awful British hand-shake!—hearty, un-sexual, and about as passionate, instinctive and spontaneous as a cold bath. We shrink from one another when we share bus seats or train seats. Fortunately, the popular press and some women's jour-nals, though not the education service, are beginning to pro-duce information about the importance of communicating

[2] Alex Comfort (ed.), *The Joy of Sex*, Quartet Books 1974, pref.

108

through touch in the interests of stable personal relationships. If they had not been handicapped by centuries of outmoded puritanism, the schools and Churches might have been on to this one long ago. The real reason why the faculty of touch is the most neglected of the five senses is, predictably, an unpleasant one: it is difficult, unless you run a brothel, to make any money out of it. Our sense of sight is exploited all day long by the visual media; our sense of hearing has been taken over by advertisers and politicians to sell us their wares; the sense of smell has been taken over by makers of perfumes and deodorants—when it has not been rendered extinct by diesel fumes and cigarette smoke. People use their voices to brow-beat us into doing their thing. The loving, pleasurable faculty of touch cannot so easily be used by others for their advantage over us. So we live in a world of anti-touch. The fist which smashes into the face, the thrown knife, the missile, the bullet, the hand which signs the paper to consign us to our fate, are anti-touch—they manipulate, they push people around, they destroy without involvement. We need, and we need desperately, the involvement, the loving involvement, of touch, the hand around the shoulder, the frank gesture of pleasure. Puritanism has always been a useful weapon in the hands of the war party, and most totalitarian regimes have been, and are, terribly restrictive about inter-personal relations. The Labour M.P., Christopher Mayhew, Chairman of the National Association for Mental Health, is reported to have said that he wondered what would happen to our social climate if the hundreds of millions spent each year on commercial advertising, on skilful appeals to vanity and greed, were spent instead extolling the simple virtues of kindness and unselfishness. Similarly honest sexuality is always opposed to oppression and the power of 'things over people'. There is something seriously wrong with a society in which people are afraid to touch others except when disaster threatens and when people are exceptionally afraid or exceptionally moved, a society which exploits all our other senses for money without conscience, and portrays shooting, stabbing and beating endlessly through its media; yet gives the personal and creative faculty of touch no scope in the enormous area between the two poles of courtship and marriage on the one hand and rape on the other.

One would hope also for a new appreciation of the arts as deeply meaningful to human experience, which is why it is so important to save them from the clutches of the exam-purveyors. We are asked to admire new towns, vast shopping complexes, missiles, computers, bridges and motorways, and new, fast cars. Some of these things are good, and we need some machines to help us, including *par excellence* those which are part of medical technology. But how much more relevant to the business of being human is the tenderness, stoicism and affirmation of Beethoven's late C Sharp Minor Quartet, or Turner's marvellous colours, or Dickens' *Pickwick* with its generous humour, or *David Copperfield*? Many people have been moved by the burst of dionysiac joy at the close of Beethoven's last symphony—the rhapsodic freedom, the abandon, of that last wild ode to joy and brotherhood and endless love. We rise to our feet at that extraordinary climax, and then go back to our trapped, humdrum lives within a closed commercial and educational system. We have yet to harness the message of art like this—to turn it, without distorting it and robbing it of artistic integrity, into ammunition for freeing ourselves. We have yet to value all this as we should. Our noisy culture is largely against such sensitivity, and our tense and anxious schools are part of that culture.

This is why poetry readings, study of the novel for pleasure, making music, and listening to music, without destructive forms of analysis; enjoying visual arts, and painting and drawing, along with the study of human movement and the pleasures of enjoying the countryside; are important to any groups seeking to achieve deeper human understanding and a deeper meaning in life; and this must be said of the essential group work to be done in schools.

By means of a great deal of informal group experience, two of education's great omissions may be compensated for: trusting growth in human relationship, and a re-consideration of our communal life-style. There is the moving story of how an unpopular girl in a secondary school class was cast in the role of an unpopular woman during an informal drama session. In the play she was expected to knock vainly at various 'doors' as she moved round the drama room, repulsed, in dramatic play, by her class-mates. Her assumed distress in this imaginary role became real distress, until at last one group, touched by her evident grief, 'let her in'. What followed was a break-through in inter-personal relations between that child and the rest of the class. In the end it is difficult to hate and reject people, even if you disagree violently with them, if you have shared a good deal with them within the overall order of informal group experience. The communication of personal needs, often hidden behind layers of timidity, aggression, or surface optimism, is a major problem. Inter-personal therapy is held up because of our fear of informal group experience. At present it is the personal columns of the popular women's magazines and the sex magazines which try to do the job we in education should share in. John Wilson talks of our inade-quate signalling of mutual needs, particularly in connection with sexual requirements. After adding that different people want different things and that we are often unsure about exactly what we want, and after dealing with love both heterosexual and homosexual, he goes on:

> Of those who wish to indulge in full intercourse, some like their sex fairly calm and relaxed, others like elements of aggression, sadism and masochism in it. Other people again want sexual activity of a more peculiar kind still, perhaps connected with certain kinds of clothing, or certain physical types of intercourse. It would be, to say the least, extremely useful and time-saving if one knew into which category people came: on this issue, at any rate, most of us feel reasonably certain about our wants. . . .
> . . . Part of the difficulty is certainly the sheer lack of an ade-quate language in which to signal.[3]

Yet about our needs, companionable, emotional, sexual, we are traditionally afraid of betraying ourselves. It's considered common and cheap to be candid. Yet almost certainly people are closer and more in need of one another, bodily and emotionally, than our present culture is prepared to admit. 'People who need people' may or may not be the happiest, but they are certainly the most alive, and 'Communication' courses of the kind presently fashionable seem to me to be farcical if they ignore the psycho-physical elements.

This is dangerous ground, though no one seems to object if

---

[3] John Wilson, *Logic and Sexual Morality*, pp.216–17. Arnold Wesker deals with an hilarious mode of sexual communication through a code language in his play *Roots* (see Act III).

advertisers dishonestly spell out their need for money. Are people's needs for others worse than their manipulation of others? Is sex worse than cold bureaucracy? I know of a university, a distinguished one in the care of many excellent and compassionate people, called upon to appoint members of its staff to governorships of schools, colleges and so forth. These posts were important policy-making posts affecting a wide area. But the wise, fair and compassionate people were defeated. For example, one large academic department had on its staff two moderately radically-minded people, with some experience of work with children and interests in comprehensive education, informal assessment methods, staff-student relations and so on. They were in no way revolu-tionary or anarchic people. One of these was offered a gov-ernorship forty-five miles from his home, so that he had to turn it down for purely practical reasons, because he could not attend evening meetings. The other was offered nothing, and so far as I know has never been offered anything. Yet right-wingers from the same academic staff, avowedly opposed to educational reforms, were appointed prolifically to key pos-itions in many institutions, where they began to dictate policy and staffing, and so far as I know still do so. The effort of the many good and compassionate men anxious to keep that university and its influence fair and just was apparently de-feated by some kind of hidden and uncontrollable caucus, and educational advance over a vast area of Britain was imperilled because of this. It was also obvious that staff who were, educationally speaking, left of centre, were often given minor, time-consuming but pettifogging commitments, apparently to keep them quiet. Arguably, manipulative activities like those characteristic of this university are far more wicked and far worse in their effects than a dozen sex orgies!

In the life-style we all need, and need to educate for, there would be no manipulation. There would be candour, and an assessment of people's real needs (as distinct from mere wants) including the needs of the Earth as well as individual needs. The sharing of one another's personal needs might lead on to a sharing of other things, perhaps into new forms of community living as ways of pooling resources and cutting down the waste of the living in the 'little boxes' to which we are accustomed, with all their mental as well as physical isolation. The Bishop of Winchester talks about 'a new kind of monastic movement which will be secular, non-celibate and non-institutional'.[4] Not that community life is for everybody, but there will be other ways, such as giving up one's car where it can be done without, or one's second car, or sharing a car; supporting and campaigning for better public transport; bringing to birth a movement which will *not* believe the things the advertisers tell us; giving up elaborate entertaining—'simple fare and a much wider circle of guests'.[5] We can stop making a fetish of food and drink as ends in themselves, and laugh out of court the people who invite us to spend overmuch precious time on fussy foods. We can refuse to buy food which has been cruelly prepared and produced. We can arrange to eat less meat, since the heavy Western demand for animal cereal feeding-stuffs is impoverishing less fortunate nations. We can boycott foreign travel to nations which imprison men without trial or torture animals for profit or sport. It would certainly mean jerking some people out of the coffee-mornings and church festivals and all the routine cosiness of life (which we all need at times) in order to discuss really important things.

What sort of people does the world need? We have no right to indoctrinate people, but we have every right and we have the duty to provide the kind of experience needful for helping people to find themselves and that human interdependence without which the world cannot survive. At present we are educating people as if they were greyhounds, running competitively in parallel tracks. We need to educate them as if they were living in a group. And not to be afraid of love.

Leila Berg has written this about A. S. Neill's school at Summerhill:

What strikes you immediately, coming from the world outside and talking to the kids at Summerhill, is that you can't tell the boys from the girls. This is important. It is not just hair-styles and jeans. The girls are so self-reliant and the boys so concerned, the girls so calmly tough and the boys so gentle. No boy's voice has that conditioned flick of off-handedness that says 'I am male'. They are interested voices, friendly and lightly generous, and their bodies are not tautly aggressive but trusting. You are

[4] John V. Taylor, *Enough is Enough*, p. 80
[5] Ibid., p. 78. See his Chapter 4, *passim*

startled when you hear their names. You begin to wonder how early children are warped in the world outside, dumped straight from the cradle on to one side of the line they must never step over, separated from one another and from their complete selves, permanently angered. Neill once said, at a progressive school conference, listening to them talk about how to keep the boys from the girls, and pressed for his opinion, 'Why don't you put up barbed wire?'[6]

The world is full of barbed wire of all sorts, and it is our job to get it down.

[6] J. Walmsley and Others, *Neill and Summerhill, A Man and His Work,* Penguin Education 1969

CHAPTER 15

Towards a New Life-style: Creative Control

It is a pertinent reflection on and of our times that audiences still have to be protected from seeing sexual intercourse on screen—an activity which surely 99 per cent of the adult population engage in at one time or another—while immorality of the political or economic variety, of business and capitalism, is not only OK but suitable. Swift would no doubt have had something corrosive to say on the subject.

These thoughts were prompted by noting that Francesco Rosi's *The Mattei Affair*, now showing at the Gate Cinema, Notting Hill, has been given a U certificate—because, one assumes, of the virtual absence of women, let alone a naked breast in its frames. The tale it unfolds, however, is a fable for our times—of how the entrenched interests of capitalism and multinational companies eliminated the man who stood in the way of their immense profits. And how, in turn, they too and the western world with them, got their come-uppance.

ARAMINTA WORDSWORTH 'The Fall of a Self-Contented Tiger',
Times Educational Supplement, 25.7.75

Come and bring the children—an entertainment for the whole family.

(Advertisement for an army display, including an attack by a rifle company, a parade of tanks supported by 105 mm Howitzer guns, and simulated battles.)

The attempt is to bring the audience into a 'feelingful' condition. One in which the simple, calm rationalist kind of talk begins to disappear, because that prevails at all the conferences of war, or among the boards of directors where men's lives are terribly exploited. We feel if we can get people to talk feelingfully, maybe the truth will come out.

JULIAN BECK, director of an 'underground' theatre group

Why, oh why, if anyone says he's going to show a dirty photograph must one immediately assume the subject matter to be sexual? Why shouldn't it be a photograph of a child seared by napalm in Vietnam? Or the obscene bloated belly of another

115

child in the final stages of starvation? A close-up shot of a penis entering a vagina isn't obscene; a close-up shot of a junkie's filthy spike entering a pin-cushion arm is. A film which shows two people writhing and moaning in sexual abandon isn't obscene. A film which shows an adolescent writhing and moaning and vomiting in the withdrawal stage of drug-addiction is even more than obscene—it is an active offence, an assault if you like upon humanity.

Parents will sit quite unconcernedly with their children in a cinema watching a film which runs the gamut of violence—head splitting swipes with iron bars, teeth being kicked out, ribs broken by boots, faces slashed with razors or burned with acid and even sexual attack 'subtly' portrayed. But if, suddenly, the film were to change to one showing the sex act those same parents would seize their kids and rush out to complain to the manager, write to their M.P. and organise a petition to close the cinema.

The obscenity of violence has escaped them.

I'll tell you what's obscene. I'll give you a glossary of obscenity and of dirty words. The following are obscene:
apartheid, witch-hunting of all sorts, victimisation, poverty, hunger, bigotry, racialism, war, disease, narrow-mindedness, ignorance (especially the invincible kind), cruelty and apathy.
The following words are dirty:
napalm, nerve-gas, bacteriological warfare, fall-out, pollution, castration, indoctrination, suppression, persecution and any other word that embodies man's inhumanity to man and nature.
I saw two obscene photographs recently. One was of youths laughing at a critically wounded soldier in Belfast, the other was of hundreds of sea-birds lying dead on an oil beach in the Shetlands. And they weren't in a Swedish magazine. *It* wouldn't print such filth.

DENNIS BURGESS, 'How Do You Define Dirt?', *She*, October 1971

Proposals for educating people towards a greater personal and inter-personal freedom do not require justification other than the greater pleasure and depth of life thus gained, provided that the freedom and privacy of others is not imperilled. But so little interested in relationships is education that the point needs making, again and again, that to make people happier in the deeper sense is an end in itself, more important than academic success or national pride or industrial development.

But there are other reasons for asserting the educational

116

task of widening personal freedom in areas like those of emotional development, friendship, sexual mutuality and cultural fellowship. Pre-eminent is the necessary shift from indignation and legislation about personal, perhaps sexual, freedom, towards indignation about other unmentioned freedoms.

We still have old-fashioned talk about 'filthiness' and 'undue permissiveness' applicable apparently to many attempts to enlarge personal relational freedom and not confined to vulgarity merely, although we have psychological evidence that some forms of permissiveness may in fact be curative in relation to various ills, including perhaps violence. Anthony Storr, psychiatrist, says. 'Whether the portrayal of sexual behaviour is harmful—I don't think there is any evidence to show this is so. I think the increase in sexual freedom has not been accompanied so far, in the young in this country at any rate—with an increase in violent feeling. Probably rather the reverse.'[1]

What is a modern theory of discipline? One could define three areas of control in human affairs; first, personal control, intellectual, emotional and sexual, best left to the genuinely educated person's own discretion (since he can be trusted more than we are accustomed to think) and left to find his own level, provided that others are not exploited; secondly, negative or outline, skeletal, control providing civil law and order, operating in such a way as to help the individual to be free not to be interfered with by any other individual and scrupulously observing existing laws to that effect; thirdly, the imaginative extension of present laws towards improved control of corruption and cruelty, still respecting personal freedom.

One might represent these three areas of control by means of a square or a box. The empty interior of the box represents the purely personal area of human relationship: it is empty because here people are not 'pushed around'; here people are not dictated to and are left free to develop their own control systems provided they respect others.

That necessary respect for others is guaranteed by the firm outline of the square or box representing the second, outline or skeletal order of public peace and decency, which is absolutely firm and necessary if people are to live orderly and peaceful lives in personal freedom, but is, in purely personal

[1] T.V. Times

matters, non-interfering and non-aggressive. (Under present conditions, largely because of our appalling neglect of education for marriage and parenthood, those responsible for this second, skeletal control are justified in invading the personal area in matters of divorce, if for example the law is needed in relation to property and the care of children.)

The third area of control is a futuristic one and might be represented by arrows pointing out from the outside of the box or square into the undefined areas beyond, or towards other, better, futuristic boxes. Here is the dynamic and exploratory extension of the law beyond existing order, still jealously guarding personal freedom, yet more and more concerned with the better control of non-personal forces in the world.

(It is very odd that we neglect future education, preferring so often to bother our children with long-distant battles, or accounts of the formation of the Earth. Much research is needed into the resistance of educational institutions to the extension of future education.)

The preceding chapter was largely concerned with the interior, the personal interior of the 'box'. At the second, negative, skeletal level our civil provision is inadequate, and getting worse. In order to be free in a purely personal manner folk need to be able to walk about the streets in peace, to be protected from murder and rape and robbery and personal assault, and to pay for and receive adequate policing of their countryside and cities. We have already noted the international disorder which plagues the world, our lack of enforceable international law. Nationally and locally we have at least a skeletal order backed up by the police, but very few people are happy about its present effectiveness. We accept a second-rate or a third-rate service, while much of the money taxed from us partly to preserve civil order is taken and used pointlessly in other directions. It is simply that our police are under-manned and under-paid. In the large and expanding commuter village where I live we have not a single resident police officer on duty—in case of need one has to be summoned from a village three or four miles away. On the whole we are a law-abiding community, but frequently people use the internal combustion engine to dash wildly and noisily round our streets, breaking the law and imperilling lives, especially of little children. But there is no one to observe, check or prosecute.

The peace of a hundred square miles can be ruined for minutes by the sound of one bomber passing. A particular niggle of my own is the insensitivity shown by the kind of people who have been turned out as 'educated' after ten or twelve years at school without any awareness of the trouble their noise causes to their neighbours. On many housing estates, even on those where people consider themselves a bit upper-crust, people use their radios and record players thoughtlessly for hours on end at full blast and in the open air, robbing others of their peace, or operate radios and T.V. sets at ferocious volume through open windows. They also leave their cars parked on pavements where adults need to walk and children need to play. It would be nice if we stopped belly-aching so much about sex and left our neighbours alone, without necessarily agreeing with them, if they decide to engage in pre-marital sex or compassionate adultery or homosexuality or experiments in group marriage, or what-ever, and just for a month or two in every year bothered a bit more about the basic discourtesies of ordinary community living, all the little erosions of the law of the land in matters of safety and consideration for others. How many people learn the law about noise in our suburbs, and their rights?

Part of the trouble is that the middle classes (especially) are too complacent. They don't want to be bothered with non-sexual social ethics. They don't wish to risk confrontation with their neighbours, even of a gentlemanly kind, and so the whole community suffers. They close their eyes to public nuisances because they prefer to think that everything in their particular locality is lovely, because they would feel upset and insecure if they admitted that life was not perfect. They wish to feel that they have been clever enough to achieve per-fection. This is why democracy, starting from the level of the local police and the local parish council, is such a sickly plant, and one so easily taken over by people with special irons in the fire, because others do not bother. We are not trained to be social watchdogs in non-sexual matters. We should be. People need to be taught how to get up petitions, how to use citizens' advice bureaux, how and how not to get help from the police, what the parish council can do and what it cannot do.

To be experts in these matters is to know how to use the existing law to the full. The third and last area of control, neglected no less by most educational institutions, concerns the extension of the law towards the eradication of cruelty and corruption. It should be concerned with the placing of appropriate pressures about the extension of a greater and deeper humanity and social order. The control of money, the control of corruption in government and in business, the control of those who would exploit the environment and cause suffering—here is the area where, beyond the present law, we need an educated citizenry to push, and push, and push! It means some shock techniques. How many people know that U.N.E.S.C.O. has reported that the world as a whole spends an average of £40 each year teaching a child to read and write, and nearly £3,000 each year in his later life on teaching him how to shoot and kill. The 'profit and loss' figures represent the amount spent on the average school pupil and the average soldier, and U.N.E.S.C.O. wants to arouse the world's conscience. How many people, as they shop round the supermarket, are aware that the pacific, beautiful whale, is hunted in the interests of the cosmetic industry, for pet foods and for detergents—not all of which are necessary and for which substitutes could be found? A whale is harpooned somewhere in the world every twenty minutes—for us, rotten us!

These are the sort of things about which we need to bully local and district councillors and M.P.s, organize petitions and get things done!

In the old days people paid their regular tithes to the Church. In our times it would help to keep the suffering and wrongness of the world in people's minds if they contracted to give a small but regular portion of their income, provided that their income was above a certain minimal level, to a cause like Oxfam or Save the Children Fund or the R.S.P.C.A. or some peace movement. It would also help if local communities, without abandoning the church flower festival/coffee-morning/whist-drive syndrome (which like all diversions is needed to some extent) sometimes set it aside to talk seriously about things. We should find enjoyment as well as profit if we did so.

Charity and goodwill is not enough. Speaking of

Bonhoeffer's theory of involvement with the world, his friend and biographer Eberhard Bethge, quotes him as saying, 'If a drunken driver is at the wheel, it is not just the minister's job to comfort the relatives of those he has killed, but if possible to seize the steering wheel.' Religion and social philanthropy are often merely ameliorative. They should be dynamic.

In the evening paper before me I read the remarks, given at a school speech-day, of a much-respected public citizen. Discipline, he says, is the jugular vein of society, and the sooner it is brought back the happier we shall be. Fine!—so long as we don't just mean more and more examinations, whatever their value, and less pleasure all round, and more blind subservience to authority. One would hope it might mean making the city quieter and more peaceful, exposing and crushing corrupt business schemes, making city councillors more sincerely accountable to the electorate, and opening the eyes of those who cause unnecessary suffering, and shaming them.

For example, how good to know that, because we had educated the electorate, a sly town council move to 'develop' part of a community on behalf of private pressure-groups and against the known wishes of people living there would be immediately disciplined and stopped. As I write, two such schemes, inadequately disciplined, are under public debate in my own corner of the country alone. How good if we could get environmentalists and caring people to form majorities on councils because their school life had made them interested in loving and caring. So much goes on which, if one thinks of conventional theories of discipline, makes one want to spew—the anarchic wickedness of nation-states which allow industrial-military cliques to sabotage disarmament proposals; the indiscipline and lack of proportion of governments which drain billions of pounds from poor people and use these to effect the union of huge, complex vehicles in outer space, while the same governments cannot be bothered to enforce the necessary discipline to provide a sane system of integrated transport on the ground; the sick morality of statesmen which permits tens of thousands of people to die painfully each year, as surely as if they had been killed by heroin or rail accidents, because governments are scared of the tobacco industry, and like, in any case, to use the money thus gained to help to balance their budgets!

Education is to see these things, and act! How good to feel that, because of our education, 'The Glorious Twelfth', when gentlemen go forth to shoot for sport birds reared trustingly to feel that they are safe, would quietly fade out as men sought their sport in more humane ways: that we could bring forth civil servants and politicians who would seek new ways towards peace: that education would force health authorities to keep the community fully informed about the many dangerous things added to our food: that governments would be at last compelled to give us pure air to breath. That is the kind of control we want, commercial discipline above all.

Just now education, in spite of I Corinthians, 13, which we read on Founder's Day, says most of the time in effect, 'Thou shalt not love', but also, 'Thou shalt compete', and 'Thou shalt do nothing about war, financial jiggery-pokery, and the enormous suffering of the Earth'. We ought to reverse all the negatives and positives in this.

CHAPTER 16

The Supreme Task

Any problem seems to have a nucleus around which all its other aspects seem to revolve. At the centre of the educational problem there is the biggest negation, the biggest omission of all: the teaching of parenthood. Because we fail to show our pupils how to bring up their own children wisely and well, so much else that we do becomes dust and ashes. This is our worst, our most unforgiveable omission. One feels as if one should beg readers to do something, anything, about this issue, even if they decide to ignore all the other issues in this book.

If we trained our pupils, young men as well as young women, in the art of parenthood, half the world's problems would be solved in a couple of generations. People would get their priorities right, their human priorities. The money-god might suffer a tactical defeat, because people would be more interested in other people and less interested in things, which is perhaps why nothing is done.

Dr Kellmer Pringle of the National Children's Bureau has campaigned for years for a square deal for children which might evolve from intelligent parent education. The work of the N.C.B. should be more widely known. Every child should be wanted, and in so far as is humanly possible should not be born unless wanted. This inescapably means a new marriage between medical and educational agencies on matters of contraception, in place of the idiotic muddle of conflicting advice, or no advice, offered at the moment to senior pupils.

The world is ravaged by people who have suffered a bad childhood. There are the spoilt children who have been given in to too much, who have been showered with material things; who had no sensible discipline at all. So they take everything as their right from others when they grow up.

There are the victims of inconsistent discipline, perhaps caught between mother and father, or parents and older relatives—children who never know where they are and suffer from permanent feelings of insecurity.

There are the children whose discipline has been too tight, too fussy, who finish up either as rebels or as zombies, because their every movement has been watched.

And there are the unloved children, unable to love in adult life, unable to relate lovingly, because they have never felt real love, care and interest. Even today, how few parents or prospective parents are aware of this crucial truth? This situation produces victims who either retreat into themselves and into the worship of things, or worse, into the terrible pursuit of revenge and power, the sticking of physical or mental knives into people. They are the street thugs, and the courts see them every day. They are also the dictators of right and left who have exterminated people by the million, and the planners who plan without caring. Our prosperous suburbs are full of unloved children, materially well off, whose parents have no time for them, and they are just turned out to play. Because they have been taught no tenderness, no close involvement, they will take, sooner or later, their revenge upon society. Many of these children have been conceived because their parents felt it their duty, a sort of social stereotyping: these children should never have been born into emotional neglect.

It is interesting and frightening to note that unloved children become interested in abstract causes rather than in people. It was noted after one of the recent Israeli–Arab wars that a significantly high proportion of young Jewish men who had fallen in the front line had been from the kind of *kibbutz* which separated mothers from children for a substantial part of the children's life. Young men who had had a normal relationship with their mother were less inclined towards acts of wild daring because they set a higher value upon their lives and their human relations. It is no denigration of bravery and patriotism to say that these facts are alarming. Religious as well as political leaders have often wished to drive barriers between parent and child in order to demand terrible sacrifices for abstract causes. In these latter days we are all sick of abstract causes; we want people, not causes. So—whenever we deny the parent-child relationship we move towards totalitarianism and hate in the world at large. Political organizations on the extreme left and the extreme right, depending for their momentum on the hatred of other classes and nations and other sects or people of other colours, are usually run by unhappy people whose attitude of permanent hate and resentment is connected with earlier experiences of being unloved and rejected. When love is denied, hatred, desire to grab and the love of power rush into the vacuum. Such people have never been given the capacity to feel sufficiently secure to be able to look with good-natured affection on people different from themselves—they cannot leap over the barriers between people to see that all life is one. Political moderation and international co-operation start in the nursery.

If I had a class of young men and women soon to leave school I would do everything in my power to help them, before they left me, to remember and understand the following (discussion group techniques would be very useful here):

(i) Always be interested in your children—it is wrong to have a child unless you can support it, love it and find time for it. It is worth sacrificing the scrupulous tidiness of a house, or the extra pin-money from a part-time job, for the sake of making your child feel that you really have time for him.

(ii) Always be encouraging—insist on minimal good order and courtesy, but never emotionally disable a child for life by making him feel small, unimportant and guilty.

(iii) Give lots of *time* to the children. Don't try and keep up the same social round, the same life-style you had before you became a parent: you can't do this without damage to the children. (This advice does not mean, however, that you can never get out for an evening.)

(iv) Talk and communicate with the child extensively. It is quite amazing to see, as I do frequently, a mother or father or grandfather sitting perhaps for an hour in a bus or a train with a child, yet apparently unwilling to speak, or answer the child's questions. But this is how he learns—warmth as well as words—by communicating extensively.

(v) Don't treat a child as your possession. He isn't, and you are in a position of trust: and while you must exercise a reasonable discipline, never impose your own dogmatisms on him and never try to dominate his thoughts and beliefs. You have no right to make him like yourself and he is not meant to be just like you.

(vi) Be child-like—which is quite different from being child-ish. Share interests and enthusiasms with your children. Remember Jesus' injunction that we should be as children, sharing the freshness and the candour of their view of life. Let the natural enthusiasm of kids wash away the adult cynicism. It doesn't matter if the neighbours think you're odd, because you're not at the squash club every night or round at the pub. Make sure that all this is consistent with, and that it is not a substitute for, a firm natural discipline. But you will probably find in the end that dialogue of this kind reduces the need for rigorous control.

(vii) Make the best possible provision for supporting your child financially, but don't kill yourself and imperil family life by sacrificing everything to money. Barbara Crane, writing recently in *Child Education*, concludes that children have suffered from rapid social change since the war. Two-car families, grandparents who live too far away, and promotion-happy dads moving house too often, assist, she concludes, in making life harder for children. Children still love their grandparents at a distance, but when these are only available by telephone they cannot be substitute parents when trouble crops up. Our modern career world has not helped to provide children with stability. And we are all scattered about far too much. Give a child stability and give him love with equal emphasis.

We can, if we wish, see this whole question within the orbit of health education. Parenthood is mental health or unhealth. An Area Health Education Officer said recently that health education was more important than history or arithmetic. The Confederation for the Advancement of State Education has asked for the inclusion of courses in parenthood in the school curriculum, and in their submission to the Schools Council Working Party on the Whole Curriculum they suggest that teenagers should extend their social service work into neighbouring playgroups, nurseries and infant schools so that they come into closer contact with small children. They also suggest that teaching on child development should be offered to children of all ability levels. C.A.S.E. believes that this might be one way of breaking 'the cycle of deprivation' which leads to generation after generation of neglected and even battered children. Dr John Howells, Director of the Institute of Family Psychiatry at Ipswich, and author of the book *Remember Maria*, has said that two children are killed by their parents each day in the United Kingdom: that many more are maimed in mind and body: that more children die at home now from ill-treatment than ever died in Dickensian workhouses. And Miss Christine Reeves, Chairman of the National Foster Care Association, has said that teaching in parentcraft is far too haphazard—'There are more courses on looking after cars than looking after children'.

Can we not, for the sake of future generations, clear some of the rubbish out of our school and college syllabuses, and give *top* priority to parentcraft? There is a splendid opportunity for colleges of education, currently suffering from a cut-back in teacher-training numbers. If they set up parent-education courses they might give tremendous support to schools, and exercise powerful leverage upon the whole social fabric.

At present the lack of official interest in parent education is suspect. At best this lack of interest is due to the fact that we are just stupid—that we just haven't thought about real education, and so we provide instead courses on cars, ancient history and gas turbines, without adequate provision for future education, partly because we lack courage to face the future honestly. At worst, the absence of courses on parenthood becomes inevitably part of that pandering to the worst elements in 'civilization' which is characteristic of so much of what passes for education. Unhappy, unfulfilled people, who find it difficult to care, are going to be the people interested in wars, fast cars, consumer fads in ridiculous variety, in conflict and in competition and in all the hectic and feverish pursuit of a lost security—not in those things which make for quietness of heart and mind. Widely-spread parent education might change our life-style, so that the world's peoples were less ready to gang up against 'the others'; less anxious to build missiles. Love leads on to love: and just there, at the beginning of that wonderful journey, the money-god sits, blocking the way.

CHAPTER 17
Planning

'Planners—the bastards!'—writes a gentleman in the course of a widely-circulated article in a family radio and television magazine. The remark is hardly fair to the many honest and worthy people in planning. But it is understandable.

Education at present is substantially concerned with the denotative and planning aspect of human life: it is about organizing things, and being cool and calculating in the process: the trouble is that without emotional maturation to accompany this type of work we get the manipulation and the planning of people as if they were articles.

It seems to me that the way we think and work in school, and the warmth or the coldness of our minds, have implications for planning. Planners have produced some pleasant garden cities. Here and there developers have done more than they need have done to provide open spaces and other recreative facilities for people. And we are tremendously good, especially in Britain, in planning rescue services and emergency operations—after things have gone wrong. Tragically, planners are also responsible for placing millions of people in miserable tower-blocks, for driving roads through people's homes and precious green fields, and for excessively dreary estates where the featureless landscape is reflected in the featureless lives of people.

Other planners have been responsible for curious methods of alienating people, confusing them. They have done this partly by giving people lots of numbers, curiously inhuman and difficult to remember—national insurance numbers, medical card numbers, post-codes, and so on. Further to this they have changed landmarks—substituting for old familiar towns and counties new confusing nomenclatures. They have abolished local authorities in favour of large, impersonal bodies a long way off. Folk used to one administrative centre find that the old offices have gone—that they are now being run by people many miles away. All this has confused and

128

worried many people, especially the elderly. The distancing of authority from the people for whom it is responsible has resulted in conclusions both hilarious and sad. Residents in a village in the north were recently told that they could not have the speed limit that they had asked for, to protect children and the elderly, 'until at least ten people have been knocked down per mile'. (Typically, the responsible distant department also stated that it would be no use imposing a speed limit that motorists would not obey.) In a neighbouring area, police and ambulance re-organization has resulted in villagers being unable to contact police quickly in emergencies—in one case such contact took almost an hour to effect—and 'rationalization' of ambulance services, organized now from a more distant point than hitherto, is thought to have contributed already to the death of one elderly woman for whom help could not arrive in time.

Incidentally, we should beware of the language of the planners, as we should beware of all official language today. We are already a good way towards the 'Newspeak' of *Nineteen Eighty-Four*. 'Rationalization' sometimes means 'sensible economies': sometimes it means 'remote empire-building for the sake of government staff at the expense of local realities'. 'Re-shaping' (of railways, for example) sometimes means 'sensible economies', but sometimes 'vandalizing and destroying for the sake of other interests'. 'Re-settlement' means, all too often, 'moving people where it's convenient for officials to put them without regard to associations and relationships'.'Public Enquiry' may mean either (i) 'A genuine attempt to test local feeling', (ii) 'A public farce with the issue decided in advance against local feeling by the Minister'. or (iii) 'A bit of local jiggery-pokery later to be over-ruled in the public's interest by an enlightened Minister or allowed to go through because the Minister is too busy'. It is with planners as with politics at large—'Defending freedom' may mean 'Defending individual loves and liberties against a real threat', but also unfortunately and/or 'Defending the interests of Western industry at the cost of consistency', and/or 'Dancing to the pipe of arms manufacturers anxious for huge profits'—it all depends. We have to educate, and we have not yet educated adequately, for our torpid electorate to wake up and scrutinize The Word.

We may note also the inconsistencies—that for all the fussy planning, all the computerized centralization, the central people-serving essentials of modern life are creaking slowly to a stop. Repair and maintenance services are getting worse: our trains are more frequently breaking down: our postal service with its slow, late, and frequently lost letters, is not a patch on the late-Victorian Royal Mail, which provided three efficient and punctual posts a day. And so with much of industry: I subscribed for a time to a mammoth, modern, computerized book-club, finally giving up in despair because, after arrangements had gone astray, it was impossible to secure any coherent reply from the computers who were apparently sending replies—I begged, and begged several times in vain, for a personal letter.

Formal methods in schools, like impersonal exam work, encourage impersonality between staff and pupils and between pupils and the world. But informal methods with appropriate group techniques can provide pupils with those face-to-face confrontations and dialogues with others which can convince them of the worth of other human beings. Too many men have been trained to adore statistics rather than care about the people to whom those statistics refer. *In Crime and Punishment* Dostoievsky comments on the convenience, the useful escape from responsibility, afforded by a purely statistical approach to life. He deals with the percentage of 'fallen women' in society:

> Haven't I seen hundreds of such girls? And what has brought them to it? Why, just that sort of thing! Anyway, to hell with it! Let them! That's how it should be, they say. It's essential, they say, that such a percentage should every year go—that way—to the devil—it's essential so that the others should be kept fresh and healthy and not be interfered with. A percentage! What fine words, they use, to be sure! So soothing. Scientific. All you have to do is say 'percentage' and all your worries are over.[1]

I have before me a letter published recently in a local newspaper. It was written by a man who had learnt casually from his evening newspaper that the 'protected' house he owned and lived in in a quiet beauty spot was to be demolished to

[1] *Crime and Punishment*, 1, iv (Penguin ed. trans. D. Magarshak)

make way for a trunk road. The authorities had not even bothered to inform him personally: he had bought the house for retirement. He had been treated as a statistic; and Dostoievsky's words remind us of more than the moral and protective effect of great literature as it seeks to humanize us. Education fails if it turns out people like the callous planners who treat people as statistics, and there is something seriously wrong with our methods if we are processing people merely to process others in their turn. Furthermore we are reminded of the dangers of educational planning, since the tendency to treat people as things, as blobs on a timetable, reveals the calculators and the statisticians at work within education itself. Schools and colleges and universities need planning, and of course they need statistics. But when the bureaucratic god takes over and we finish merely by counting heads or by counting examination passes without considering all the inner human issues involved, then we might as well shut up shop and go home. The prestige of the school or college or university, or merely the bureaucrat's delight in committee-spinning—all these can reduce people to nothing.

Much of our teaching needs to be unplanned, and that means un-planned, with the planning taken out of it. We still need a good deal of planning, but we also need plenty of unplanned experiences and dialogues and explorations, for only through these can the human spirit be kept alive. Then we should have more chance of turning out people who will be the right and not the wrong sort of planners: who will not plan callously after being bought off by private pressure-groups, or plan merely to please themselves with planning; but plan for people. They will be warm-hearted people who feel warmth towards the community and towards the country they live in, its cities and its countryside: they will often have come from warm families and from caring schools. If our schools and colleges and universities are like factories we shall increase the flow of the cold planners and politicians who use people as if they were objects. Conversely, a campaign to make education warmer and kinder and more person-centred must, in the end, regenerate and humanize the present largely heartless world of committees.

131

CHAPTER 18

Linking Up With the Churches

In the Preface some claim was made to the effect that this book was 'about' religion. Any reader might be forgiven for thinking that I had stalled on this one, and might complain that nothing had appeared except a series of waspish attacks upon the Churches. Unless, of course, you take the view that the whole business of making the world less destructive and more compassionate is a religious activity, a view I would myself take.

In the last chapter I risk the hope that we may see a new goodwill movement in favour of a compassionate education, bringing together parents, teachers and pupils. One might hope with equal confidence for very significant help from the tremendous fund of goodwill preserved within the Churches, and perhaps not within the Christian Churches alone.

The existence of this reservoir of great kindness has never been more evident than it is today. In recent years the Churches have shown a new practicality in their work (for example) for Christian aid to underdeveloped countries, in their work for local charities, and in the quality of the kind of contribution made by religious men and women to other forms of social work in great variety.

The college where I am employed bears on its crest the proud motto, 'That they might have life and have it more abundantly'. The college's Christian foundation is reflected in the care shown by my colleagues, by Christians, and by those who hesitate to make a full Christian commitment, to students in their difficulties and also to their fellows on the staff. We are all influenced by a religious tradition which helps us towards a climate of helping and understanding as much as towards one of judgement and discipline.

Somewhere within that delicate balance—between the needs of discipline and judgement, and the needs of per-missiveness, new understanding and change—lies the key to the great difficulties and the great possibilities facing the

Church as a reformist force in social and educational affairs. The Church always has been and always will be torn between those who think that ritual is more important than practical affairs; those for whom elaborate ritual is the mainspring of social and practical action; those whose lack of interest in ritual is replaced by little more than a mechanical and authoritarian interpretation of scripture; and those whose lack of interest in ritual goes along with a concern for practical action and for a dynamically-changing concept of the religious ethic in modern times.

Just before the Second World War there was a significant growth of interest in the Church as a social force. The work of Dr J. H. Oldham and his Religious Book Club, the influence of the great Archbishop Temple, and of Dr Bell of Chichester and of other leading clergy, the reformist climate engendered by the war itself and men's hopes for a new world—these and many other things made people hope for a new, pastoral, practical Church which might sometimes step outside its own buildings to become, in Matthew Arnold's phrase, a national society for the promotion of goodness. These hopes were revived and strengthened for a short time under the tragically short reign of Pope John.

During the last decade or so our hopes have not been strengthened. Daily rituals go on inside our Anglican Cathedrals while the jet-fighters scream overhead and crooked politicians are active in the towns outside, but few people seem to connect. The Papacy, against the advice of many of the best minds in the modern Roman Church, has revealed a tendency to turn again towards mysticism and towards an unhelpful and conservative (and sometimes distinctly brutal) view on sexual matters, although the present Pope has shown much interest in the cause of peace. The Churches seem fatally split between an all-absorbing interest in ritual of the most elaborate kind for its own sake (almost as theatre), and on the other hand a more or less mechanical form of evangelism, which is usually sincere, but relies brainlessly on the mechanical interpretation of scripture. Very oddly, evangelists who rely most heavily on the doctrine of the Holy Spirit as a force to change the hearts and minds of men, and involve themselves often in highly-emotional and charismatic forms of group experience, seem to have no faith at all in a creative spirit which might re-create truths anew in each generation and is not bound to a series of once-for-all rules which are inept in modern life. Sometimes at home, and more particularly abroad, extreme forms of evangelism consider ethical behaviour exclusively in terms of sex and drugs. Groups of this kind often have the powerful financial and moral backing of business men whose own attitudes are belligerent, competitive and war-like. As we have seen, the obsession with sexual purity affords the usual smoke-screen behind which big business can get on with its usual nastiness. The Devil is very good at providing decoys for us: it is his cleverest game. We are continually being warned by evangelical people about the 'sin' of giving way to the lack of control, even to the madness, of love; whereas the greatest sin is the madness of money, which blinds all who give way to it to the social and environmental consequences of what they are doing.[1] Even those well-intentioned people who have brought the phrase 'moral pollution' into common parlance have done so at the cost of deflecting attention from financial and environmental wickedness.

Every now and then we are jerked out of those mechanical modes of thought which Matthew Arnold hated so much. It was before the last war when that great Christian, Dorothy L. Sayers, remarked—before it was fashionable to say such things—that if every man in Britain slept one night with his neighbour's wife these acts would cause less harm to the Kingdom of God than routine corruption active in industry and politics every day. There was the consultant psychiatrist on T.V. who tried to get our moral hysteria under control by remarking quietly that adultery was the silliest reason for divorce. There was Dr John Robinson in the mid-sixties with his existential or situational ethic based on a law of love which could, in certain situations, transcend the letter of the law—an ethic vehemently denounced by the Roman Church. As I write there are hopeful signs; that ritual may be seen, even where it is elaborate, as a springboard for action; that a new concern for the enormity of the waste and corruption of our industrial society is beginning to be thought about in Christian terms; and one or two of the Church leaders at the very top

[1] The familiar phrase 'motorway madness' has therefore a deeper shade of meaning.

seem to be helping us to move forward in this context. To re-define sin; that is the task; within a compassionate and caring society, not without discipline, but with a realistic and perceptive discipline within which people can have a more abundant life. What an ideal!—and one which can sometimes make one weep because of its seeming unattainability.

New ideas are circulating, people are beginning to think in new ways. The monthly parish talk in the church magazine is not always now about the church decorations, or infant baptism, or the doctrine of sanctification. It is sometimes about pollution, or over-population, or about problem families. New types of discussion-group are springing up, sometimes meeting in people's homes instead of on church premises. Some of theses groups welcome Christians and non-Christians as equals and fellows, endeavouring to talk out religious problems undogmatically and with the emphasis on communication rather than upon conversion. Surely in movements like these, and in some of the books now being written by prominent clergy, and in some of the practical work being done by Christians towards the relief of suffering—work in which to some extent they must jettison preconceived Christian judgements of the old-fashioned kind—there is hope for religious involvement in the work of humanizing education also.

In the light of the recommendations made in the next chapter one looks hopefully for help from the Churches at various levels and in various ways.

If we are going to try to get together groups at grass-roots level—teacher, pupil, parent groups—we are going to be short of spiritual capital if we leave out the Christian contribution. It would be good if clergy, lay leaders, and ordinary folk with some kind of religious vocation, came in as a steadying influence, to help perhaps simply in private meetings in private houses, meetings in schools, action committees—what you will—to engage generally in the job of mutual education. They should not be there to beat their own drum or to convert anybody, but to wash other people's feet, as Jesus is said to have done—to help those who need help, and help because it is Christian to help: simply that.

Then we need help from Church institutions already involved in education—Church schools. Church colleges, and so on. To help will not be a matter of teaching and enforcing Church dogma: rather the reverse. Church schools have spent too much time teaching dogma, with the result that they have produced unnecessary fear and guilt in their pupils and intensified the risk of sectarian division, war and murder beyond their doors, as in the tragic case of Northern Ireland. It isn't the task of Christian education to give its pupils a set of instructions to be followed mechanically under all conditions, as if they had no dynamic creative gift in themselves, as if they were babes. The task of religious education is to fashion a religious life-style, and to nurture in people that creative spirit of love that will help them to grow up and live wisely without a rule-book. Therefore the life-style of a good Church school or college should be friendly to the kind of new courses and new ideas which a humane education requires. If the Christian institution is a family with a good family feeling it will not over-stress its students, nor harrow them with unnecessary guilt and fear, but it will encourage a growth of caring; and far from turning people out obedient to prescribed orders in all their mechanical detail, it will make them suspicious; compassionately questioning all those cunning and inhumane assumptions which society forces upon them. We are back to 'love and awareness', Huxley's twin virtues. These are also the virtues of a Christian, who is called upon not only to be a good man, but also not to be a fool. To question, to question, to be suspicious, is of the essence of religious education, so that our pupils can grow up to do without us, relying absolutely on the law of love. 'Duty and reverence'—yes, but new occasions teach new duties, and the ultimate reverence must be for life, not for legalisms.

Thirdly, one would hope for help from distinguished Church leaders, not only because they would encourage a new life-style and experimentation with new courses in Church schools and colleges, but because they might give diplomatic and political support and leadership to teachers and parents and lecturers and pupils struggling to free themselves from old procedures. If a campaign for a new humanity in education could have the backing of one or two bishops who would speak for it both locally and nationally, we might be more than half-way towards success. And what about a more vigorous integration of Church leadership with political affairs, of the kind more common about the end of the nineteenth century, and then again about the middle of this century? Why should not Church leaders, without party involvement, advise people as to how they should vote, and why they should vote, and why they should protest?

Our main task remains, to get old cruelties out of schools and out of higher education, and get new courses and attitudes in, and if necessary to resist old orthodoxies hostile to these. It would be reasonable to expect that sincere Christians, and Jews, and other committed religious people, would show special sympathy towards any attempts to save the arts, literature especially, from the exam-grubbers and the comprehension tests. After all, we have in the Bible, and in other religious books, some of the world's greatest literature, some of the world's greatest poetry. The Authorized Version of the Bible is one of the world's literary treasures. How can the Christian be at ease, if he feels something of the power and beauty, for example, of the Book of Isaiah, when he knows that great literature is being mangled daily in classrooms up and down the length and breadth of the land?

CHAPTER 19

Living With Half a Mind

This book has developed into one long plea—not, it is indeed hoped, a monotonous and boring one—not only for love, but also for imagination, in our colleges and schools. This plea is for the use of the whole mind, intellectual and emotional, detached and involved; for only when the whole mind is alive can imagination work and creativity operate. And the trouble is that so many institutions formally connected with education and with morality behave as if they had, at best, only half a mind.

The Churches appear to operate with half a mind because they are committed to observances and traditions which have in many cases become mechanical and lost their meaning; because their conceptions of sin are changing too slowly, because they are still caught up in the catastrophic anti-sex syndrome which blinds them to the perception of so many other forms of sin. In view of what has been said above about co-operation between education and religion, I make these assertions regretfully. They are not true about a growing minority of Christian people. The truth remains, however, that most church-goers still would not understand if you told them to demonstrate outside a shop selling war comics or war toys instead of demonstrating against soft porn; or to run a campaign against the American-style hunting magazines which have recently appeared in this country; threats to life, charity, and even survival, have not yet been imaginatively perceived.

The education machine appears to possess only half a mind; because it continues to brow-beat students into endless grubbing-up of inert facts and inert ideas, and continually refines the examination machine without asking the basic questions about examining. It deliberately ignores so much that is practical, necessary and urgent for the survival of mankind. And it operates, if not mindlessly, at least with only half the mind when it tries to set up standards. A Department

138

of Education research group is, as I write, working on an assessment of performance in schools which is due to start in 1978. Its comments on the teaching of English are revealing. For example, primary children would be looked to for expressive writing, but for 16-year-olds 'the emphasis has shifted towards writing in which the pupil's feelings are suppressed'.[1] It identifies four levels of comprehension: to understand and recall items of fact; to précis; to infer and attribute cause and effect; and to evaluate style and tone in writing. There is no encouragement for the refining and nourishing of the emotional life, no radical criticism of society, no love, no care. Half the mind is out of action, and one despairs as one reads these coldly clinical tasks, which are ideal for producing unequally developed people to fit without questioning anything into an unfeeling, mechanical society.

Only half-aware also is the mental state of the governments of the world to which we look for ultimate guidance and ultimate discipline. Petty laws proliferate, many of them unenforceable. While the desperate need to put every effort into international peace-making stands before them as high as Mount Everest, our Members of Parliament and the police, and the courts which enforce their edicts, are busy persecuting adult homosexuals north (but not south) of Berwick-on-Tweed, or making sure that fish and chips are wrapped separately on Sundays.

All three great areas of human endeavour largely ignore the fourth area, the world of the arts. If they took note of it they would all be wiser, for the world of the arts is the world of imagination, of creativity and change, and ultimately of love and of beauty. One cannot enjoy Shakespeare, Dostoevsky, Ibsen, Shaw, Whitman, without learning to ask questions. All the time the arts use the whole mind—its constructional, intellectual and even clinical side, but also its capacity for colour, feeling and love. One could put a potentially extended commentary simply and succinctly by saying that a person with his whole mind alive to artistic feeling would be able to appreciate, while the average churchman would only

---

[1] Bob Doe, 'No Marks for Objectivity', *The Times Educational Supplement*, 3.12.76. I am assured by Her Majesty's inspectors for whom I have great respect that this report does not represent any kind of solid body of opinion within the Department of Education and Science.

condemn, Schubert's *Delphine*, which is about the ecstatic
love of a married woman for a much younger man who
is not her husband; that the international statesmen of
the world do not seem to have grasped with their whole minds
what Britten was saying in his War Requiem or Beethoven in
his ninth symphony; that for many educational administrators, Blake is as if he had never lived, and E. M. Forster's
Howard's End as if it had never been written.

The unique nightmare of the late twentieth century will
only yield to organs of religion, government and education
which possess those priceless gifts of the imagination; love,
flexibility and creativity. The hard truth is that these cannot
be nourished without radical changes in the curriculum. And
another hard truth is that this may not be done without
dogged resistance on the part of people or groups as yet
unformed and unidentifiable to those who want us to act as
though we had no minds, or, at best, no feelings.

CHAPTER 20

Proposals for Change

This book has argued for an education very different from anything most people recognize as education. In our stodgy society with its manifold bottlenecks, both social and bureaucratic, even small changes are so difficult to make that the effort required may well appear to exhaust the would-be reformer. Moreover we are faced with a terrible closed system. A differently-structured and humane education needs people used to a new life-style, but we can't teach people about a new life-style until educational structures change to permit new teaching. 'They' have got us where they want us, every time. Or have they?

But we may at least suspect that 'They' exist. To be made more suspicious as well as more loving—Aldous Huxley's 'Love and awareness'—is where we start: to have a mind like a knife, or a microscope, not to be like an educational sponge soaking brainlessly up all the details recommended by a syllabus.

Otherwise we have to realize that we may be able to do nothing, except in so far as a common purpose in wishing to make education humane brings people together in new relationships. There is also a hope, beyond this, that small cells, or discussion-groups, developing in a relatively unorganized way in people's homes and in churches, may eventually work like the leaven in the lump.

But it is important to believe in the possibility if not in the certainty of being able to do more than these things. There *are* plenty of good men in local and in national government and in educational administration; there *are* influential key people willing to help, if only unobtrusively; there *are* M.P.s who put rightness and kindness above political careerism. One of the glories of life in this hideously corrupt world, once it has been seen for what it is, is to find so much unexpected goodness, so much conscience. Love lingers. And so without killing ourselves and denying our own personal relationships, which may be all we shall ever achieve, there are things to push for, using all the help we can get. With some over-laps, they resolve themselves into: (1) Direct proposals for government action, something to press M.P.s about; (2) Proposals for change within school and in higher education; (3) (Perhaps most controversial) proposals for working with parents and pupils in order to force upon education by all peaceful democratic means a realistic education designed to secure the survival of our children.

1. Proposals for direct government action
A Commission on the effect of the School Examination Boards on the appreciation of the Arts
We need to press urgently for an official government enquiry or commission, carried out, as has been suggested above, in the light of the money spent on the propagation of culture in the community at large. If the school examining boards are ruining literature, the visual arts, music and other things, so that children dislike them for the rest of their lives, we might as well agree that $X=0$ and save government money at present spent in subsidizing the arts. Indeed the proposals in this chapter must begin and finish with the great examining boards. This book has been very critical of those boards (some would say over-critical), and it must be said that some (especially some of the younger boards) are less injurious than others, and that there are involved in the work of every board many good, compassionate and sincere men and women. This is not to say that even good men and women are fully conscious of what they are doing, or of what their colleagues are doing, or of the force of the mental cliché which implies that what they are doing is right. The examination boards make up a built-in industrial system, which on the whole carries on because it has carried on, because it is self-perpetuating. Generally the boards function as spiritual Pentagons, purveyors of spiritual violence and stress, their victims the sensibilities, and sometimes the health, of thousands upon thousands of young people.

To say this is to risk being scoffed at and to be asked to prove the case. If Her Majesty's government is concerned about the welfare of the young, it should ask the examining boards themselves to prove the case wrong, and a totally impartial commission, on which children are adequately and democratically represented, should take the evidence directly from the schools.

Mild reluctance to appoint such an enquiry would indicate lack of interest in young people. A persistent, or extreme, reluctance to appoint such an enquiry would indicate a political reluctance to contemplate the possibility of pupils in their mid-teens who are not cowed, over-worked and preoccupied.

2. Change within schools
Parenthood
Courses in parenthood should be sympathetically and warmly taught in all senior schools. Such courses should include visits to nurseries, to court-rooms, to children in care, perhaps even to Borstals, so that the effects of a wrong up-bringing are brought home to children themselves at first-hand. These courses should involve boys as much as girls. Here is a splendid opportunity for the reformed colleges of education, at present suffering from a decline in the numbers of students training for teaching. If they could put on wise and sympathetic courses in parenthood they might be able to turn out adequate numbers of trained counsellors to work with teachers in schools.

Counselling
Much, much more money must be spent in the schools on the provision of adequate counselling services. They should include psychiatric back-up work preferably undertaken by psychiatrists interested in young people and sympathetic to them and specially trained. Advice on sexual hygiene and contraception should be freely available without embarrassment. Our present attitudes are ridiculous. We have failed to train parents, in a past generation, to take their responsibilities seriously. At the same time we refuse to help the children of those parents when they cannot get advice and guidance at home, so, as usual, the kids lose both ways.

Parenthood and general counselling: everything should be subservient to these in terms of time, money and staffing. We have got to start supporting children, not merely demanding things of them.

Life-style—leisure
A new element of relaxation and of education for leisure is
important in senior education. This element, present in good
primary schools, is lamentably lost in the upper reaches of
school life. All this means a new stress upon creativity,
therapeutic drama, art and writing, much more work in small
groups: and timetabled time for these things. The arts must be
rescued and put to their proper use as enrichments of the
human spirit: these attitudes will then carry over into life
outside school. Just now the vandalism on buses, the scrawlings on walls, the drunkenness and the vulgarity and basic
poverty of ideas for spending leisure are as much our failure as
those of the young people we blame. We need a race of young
people who will not only enjoy their parties and their occasional sowings of wild oats, but also walking, mountaineering,
enjoying science, inventing things, helping the disadvantaged,
painting, writing, making music, undertaking social and political research even. And these things could be enjoyed as much
as the bashing up of property. It is our stuffy teaching which
blocks up these avenues of interest.

A divided syllabus
If the things above need to be done, and if we can persuade
enough people that they need to be done, time will have to be
found for them. So there would inevitably have to be fewer
academic subjects to be taken after the age of about eleven, or
at the latest, about thirteen. *We have to think in terms of a
divided syllabus—partly for social education (without formal
examination) and partly academic.* We come back again to the
examining boards, and, beyond them, to entry requirements
for higher education and certain professions. Again the situation looks hopeless, because so many employers and a
lamentable number of teachers and lecturers, *simply look for
numbers of subjects instead of for quality. But, somehow,
potential employers have got to be made to understand that
quality is what counts.* Fortunately many universities and
polytechnics and colleges are now keen on looking for one
or two really good academic attainments, not for a rag-bag;
plus an outgoing personality.

What is needed, therefore, is the firm concept of *a divided
syllabus*, to give rhythm and variety to school life. Something

144

like one-third or one-half of the time, after the age of 11 or 12, could be devoted to a very small number of academic subjects, probably not more than two or three in number, not over-packed with material, done well because they are really enjoyed and appreciated and represent a definite pupil choice. The other half of the time could be given over to social education, without formal examination, designed to assist the humane and disciplined development of the pupils as persons. Prominent amongst topics within this second category will be:

Education for survival
The preservation of peace and what may be done to preserve it, the dangers to survival from the petrol engine and the cigarette and other lethal things; social studies designed to increase responsibility to oneself and to the environment. Pupils must be shown before they leave school how to feel responsibility and how to exercise responsibility towards themselves and others.

Higher education
One would very much hope that creative methods of learning and teaching would spread upwards into higher education, and might help to rescue the more formal academic disciplines from the debilitating grind and joylessness which characterizes some of them. So deeply entrenched is the puritanism of the English-speaking peoples that we find it difficult to conceive of higher education, supported by rates and taxes, unless the young people we are supporting are going though a hell of a time. We have to educate ourselves to believe that there is some point in a healthy balance between relaxed creativity and academic rigour in higher education, and some point in turning out people who will be happier and more balanced persons because of higher education—not merely little know-alls. It is not enough to leave the personal maturation of students to their talk over coffee-cups.

Academic Education: Departments and Colleges of Education
One area of academic life in particular need of reinvigoration is the area of academic Education. Many students have been helped by good Departments and Institutes of Education in universities, but the prevailing impression of Education as an

academic subject is of a quite alarming aridity. This is a pity, because one would hope that at the supreme level of the university, education, whether with a small letter or a capital letter, would be at its most dynamic, most inspired and most deeply and compassionately in touch with life. Some mention has already been made of the near-incredible academic remoteness of the syllabuses of some advanced diplomas and degrees in Education, finishing up all too often with dreary statistics or historical obscurities or linguistic minutiae—which is not to say that M.Ed.s and PhD.s in Education do not sometimes produce useful results. More commonly open to question is the traditional syllabus for the post-graduate Certificate in Education (formerly known as the Dip.Ed.) used in the training of graduate teachers, and reflected also in the education programme of many polytechnics and colleges of education. The traditional menu of compulsory Philosophy of Education, History of Education, and Psychology of Education, with Method (classroom practice) thrown in as a kind of Cinderella subject with less academic *cachet* attaching to it, is hardly adequate in the modern world. As usual we do everything for the wrong reasons—the real reason for the heavy emphasis on Philosophy, Psychology and History is that these topics look academically respectable. This procedure has nothing to do with the welfare of students. Surely Environmental Studies, or rather a course in Environmental Responsibility, together with studies in responsible social action of a democratic nature, and profound and caring studies in parenthood and in the child-teacher relationship would, together with methods of teaching an academic specialism, make up a more realistic menu for future education.

There seems to be some point in expecting intending teachers, during a very brief and hurried year, to know something of the theory of education, and something too of educational psychology, which remains one of the more popular subjects in the post-graduate certificate course when it is taught well. But there is not time for too much even of these, and there are higher priorities. Philosophy, and History (the most unpopular subject), and Statistics and Linguistics and so on, would be better as optional topics taken by those students who are really interested in them.

Helping People

Education teaching in many universities is unsatisfactory because it has got tied up with the wrong kind of seeking for prestige, and so has dissociated itself from the reality of the world and the cares of the world. Those responsible should forget academic notoriety, and think instead of service: all things would be added unto them of they did.

Basic skills
This section has been concerned mainly with the possibilities of reform in terms of syllabus and matter taught in schools. It may be worth attempting to allay the fears of those who feel that a much-restricted number of academic subjects would involve a neglect of basic conceptions such as language and number. There would be compensation from the informal area into the academic area. In other words, a young man or a young woman who has dropped English Language, or Mathematics, in order to take only two or three subjects he really cares about—after the age of say, 13—will be inevitably involved in language and in number in his environmental and social studies within the non-academic area, naturally, and with motivation.

As I close this section, after a plea to release children from the rag-bag of numerous 'O' levels, I feel a cold shudder down my back! What about a formal exam for everybody at the age of 13! The forces of reaction are always waiting to pounce!

3. Pupils, teachers and parents: proposals for action
The big question remaining in my mind and in the minds of many readers will be—how do you get action and change in these matters? And it is a difficult problem.

The help of sympathetic individuals in positions of influence must never be underestimated. Nor should the quiet, democratic work of people working for change on boards and committees. For myself, however, I see no general way forward without a new consensus of feeling and co-ordination of effort between pupils, teachers and parents.

We need action both within and outside the educational set-up: we need to save our children from exploitation outside and within the educational system. We need also to educate ourselves. I see a new grass-roots movement involving parents and teachers and pupils, and, one would hope, the teachers' unions too, as a great exercise in reform and dialogue. But I see it even more as a quite new kind of adult education. Pupils are not alone in needing to be educated about the modern world. Many parents have shuttered minds, and many teachers also.

A Campaign for Humanity in Education. A spontaneous campaign which would involve us all in caring for the deeper happiness of the kids.

A Campaign for Humanity in Education. It would, if necessary, organize legal and peaceful resistance to inhumanity, the inhumanity of some examining boards, and of some educational authorities—and it would educate itself to boycott anyone, or any institution, involving itself in unnecessary cruelty or strain. It would be adult education at its best.

This is not Marxist militancy. I am not interested in barricades and class warfare (there is a much more serious war going on—war against children). I hold no brief for the awful rigidity of the extreme political left, as bad and as dangerous and as old-fashioned as the extreme right-wing rigidity of some governors, head teachers and education authorities. C.H.E. means human and relational dialogue, flexibility, willingness to change, willingness to learn from one another, willingness to think new things. But it also means getting on the side of the kids whom we are really supposed to be serving all the time. What a challenge to us all, and what a challenge to the principalities and powers arrayed against us!

It would be a tremendous step forward in community education if we could get teachers and pupils talking together out of school, parents and children talking together across the communication gap, and teachers and parents talking about things not entirely centred upon exam results, which is the usual excuse for their meeting. And how good if the National Union of Teachers and the other teachers' unions—and the journals of these unions indicate the presence of many forward-thinking minds—left the topics of status and salaries to talk with all others concerned about the personal welfare of the children. British teachers have recently been upgraded money-wise: this would be a splendid time for them to give financial concerns a lower priority for the moment.

It would be more than helpful if at this stage progressive Church leaders and members 'came over to Macedonia to

help us' in our new task of developing grass-roots responsibility. We have heard enough of grass-roots protest, and
we have heard enough of back-lashes against other people.
Here is a chance for a grass-roots protest on behalf of people
and against things.

The need would appear to be for protest on two fronts. On
behalf of the children we must get together to bombard politicians, both local and national, about war and peace and
disarmament, about the environment—and not simply on vast
cosmic issues which people simply cannot visualize in tangible
terms. The obvious wastage of public money on a silly project
around the corner which we can all see, the obvious official
sabotaging of efforts to recycle glass and paper or to avoid
wastage in packaging[1]—the children themselves could be
working on this sort of theme in school. Politicians get away
with so much because of our apathy. Let's all get out of our
watertight boxes, people, teachers, pupils, and start making
people accountable to us.

More difficult is the question of protest against matters in
the educational system itself. The most intractable problem of
all is the humanizing of the vast examination system.

If we rely on the force of public opinion to change the
examination system it may take a hundred years. And the
need is so urgent. We need to cut down the rag-bag of 'O'
levels at 16, we need to humanize the remaining exams so that
they become tests of creativity rather than of capacity for
long-suffering, and do not straddle the whole curriculum; and
we need to work towards the elimination of the formal exam
in favour of humane assessment methods.

One possibility would be to force the examining boards to
be more humane by withdrawing labour from them, or by
threatening so to do. They rely heavily on teachers and lecturers, and on students—the latter frequently for administrative work. The students need the money to get through the
vacations and the teachers and lecturers use the money to
inflate their income, raise their standard of living and perhaps
pay for expensive holidays abroad. Some of the teachers and
lecturers and some of the students will genuinely need the

---

[1] A charitable body in my own area has recently had to destroy several tons of
waste newsprint, collected laboriously as a means of raising money, because no one
would buy it for reprocessing.

extra emoluments. But I doubt whether they all do. At a time when a newer and simpler life-style seems more and more appropriate, it is also appropriate to appeal to some of these employees and their families, as a matter of principle, to withdraw labour, or to threaten to do so, in the interests of children.

Failing this—and I make the suggestion with great hesitancy and yet with conviction—if there is any issue on which a strike would be justified, except perhaps on the issue of the protection of the environment, or on the issues of peace and war—then this is it: a parents' and teachers' strike, one would hope with the backing of the teachers' unions, to end the cruelty of the examination rat-race in schools. This would inevitably involve pupils—possibly as part of the protest. We have had strikes for the lowest of reasons in Britain and elsewhere, for trivial reasons and selfish reasons; and lots of strikes for money; if we must have a strike let it be, for once, for humanity. We are, here, on the wretched fringe of lawlessness, because it is an offence to withdraw children from school without due cause. Lawlessness is a terrible thing and it is no part of this book to advocate civil disobedience. Therefore it might be more appropriate if work were to continue in school outside the examination nexus, whilst we force the examination people to rediscover their own humanity. These proposals can therefore fittingly end with some remarks of Eric E. Robinson about cold bureaucracy, which we take so readily for granted. His words oddly remind one—though he does not necessarily write as a Christian—of words of Jesus and Paul, and of that ethic of love above law which certain administrators, even those whose specialism happens to be theology, seem to have forgotten:

> There is no substitute for sheer humanity, sentimental though it may sound. By this I mean an awareness of and a concern for what is happening to people. It is always possible to score a point in a conference on higher education by commenting that no one has mentioned students.
>
> Within the hierarchies of higher education preoccupation with 'bigger' issues than the experience of students is only too easy. A useful discipline in any academic committee is to keep asking what effect our decisions will have on what actually happens to students.

150

And surely it is never sufficient, when a decision is challenged, to reply that all regulations have been satisfied and all the rules have been obeyed.[2]

The things set out in this chapter need to be done. Not all of them will get done soon, and some may not get done at all. But if nothing gets done two things will be proved beyond any doubt; our apathy as teachers and parents, the final vote of no confidence to be passed in favour of ourselves; and the triumphant intent of the Establishment to keep us as we were for reasons which have no connections with our own well-being.

[2] Eric E. Robinson, 'The Buffoons of Blind Bureaucracy', *The Times Higher Education Supplement*, 25.7.75

CHAPTER 21

Afterthoughts

It would not be fitting to end this book on a negative note. Its last chapters were sketched out soon after I had heard Mahler's Eighth Symphony, 'The Symphony of a Thousand', as performed at the opening night of a recent series of London's Promenade concerts. The medieval Latin hymn, *Veni, Creator Spiritus*, with which Mahler's symphony opens, expresses a prayer for divine light, a belief in man's pursuit of love, and a conviction that the universe is able to respond to man's aspirations. Mahler was not afraid of feeling. 'Imagine', said Mahler of this work, 'that the whole universe bursts into song'. I have often thought, with despair, of those words while supervising arts students sweating miserably over novels and poems during three-hour papers.

The whole trouble is that education, for so much of the enormous amount of time it demands of us and of our growing children, is light-years away from any kind of creative experience. If there are significant areas in which it is creative and inspirational and forward-looking these are mainly in primary education; and in science, especially in Biology and Astronomy, where at the present time there is the excitement of creative discovery. Our record on the arts side is dismal in comparison. The creative arts flourish, when they can, principally outside schools and universities. It was George Bernard Shaw who said long ago that university education reduced the arts to pedantry, though mercifully this is not true of all colleges and universities today.

Veni, Creator Spiritus. Mahler's notion was of something loving and reconciling, to bind men together as his music bound together that audience at the Royal Albert Hall; something dynamic and flexible, and with capacity for growth and change; something healing and constructive; and something that was not only theoretical and metaphysical but also practical and earthy. And that spirit and that vision make up a standing rebuke to an education which is cold and clinical,

152

static and repetitive and capable only of trivial change, divisive and geared towards war, practical mainly in the service of money, and destructive of human sensibility. Instead of being like a unifying experience, education is like a continuous programme of those quizzes and contests to find the best 'brain', which have confirmed the public idea of education as being something to do with being like an encyclopedia, instead of being a full human being. It bears as much relation to real life as do the stuffed animals in the backs of our cars, and in our children's toy-boxes, and the lovable animals in the television cartoons and puppet shows, to the real, living animals, suffering silently in their millions.

Some of us entered teaching hoping for two things—that we could transmit to others the enthusiasm and enjoyment we felt in scholarship, and while doing so help to train ladies and gentlemen, in the finest senses of those words, and so advance social progress. We find now that we are processing little human computers to fit, without questions being asked, into a violent and selfish society. Education, the education we fought for and prized so much ourselves, is in effect, if not by intent, a prostitute to that society. We should like to return to the dignity and humanity which once seemed possible. We are tired of being, all the time, harried, jostled. 'Feed my sheep.' 'Feed my lambs.' But you cannot, when a dozen committees, a dozen Chief Examiners, are pulling at your back collar.

All over the world children are crying. The blame is partly ours in education—they have asked for bread, and we have given them stones, and the world they have inherited is full of stones, full of guns. We should stop the timetable sometimes, and listen to those cries. We don't give them a satisfactory answer, in their demand for a more abundant life, if we give each child ten 'O' levels, three family cars, and a nation with the greatest armed might.

At the close of a book which has complained a great deal, if unavoidably, and has sometimes been very sad, words which Mahler set for his Credo provide a relevancy far better than any words of my own:

Come, Creator Spirit, Kindle our senses with thy Light, Pour thy love into our hearts.

153

Appendix A

Sample Research Material for Chapter 5
Stratford protest over rail cuts

Stratford upon Avon, rated by some as Britain's second most important tourist centre, may be profitably quaint in some ways, but it reckons it can do without British Railways making it even quainter.

It is cut up about being cut off from direct rail links with major cities and towns. It has, as a prime example, no through daily services to London. And, as a surprised and mortified Stratford upon Avon points out, even Moreton-in-Marsh has that.

Last night a deputation made a protest to the divisional passenger manager of British Railways. The theatre, the birth place, the member of Parliament, the Mayor and corporation, the shopkeepers, hoteliers, caterers, and publicans complained that the way things seemed to be going, Stratford would become merely a branch line terminal.

A calendar of cuts, drawn up by the local Chamber of Trade, showed that since the heydays of 1962, when you could get a through coach to London—the coach was hooked on to the Birmingham–London train at Leamington Spa—all Sunday train services have been stopped; the late night theatre train to Birmingham has been withdrawn; various other services have disappeared, and last month the connecting trains to Leamington for London services were heavily reduced.

British Railways' short answer is that Stratford services have been 'modified to bring them into line with demand'. Stratford concedes that of the 350,000 visitors to Stratford each year, 80 per cent travel by road. But it argues: 'It is obvious that the provision of convenient rail services would reduce congestion on the main roads and in the streets and car parks of Stratford.'

It is not only the tourists Stratford is concerned for, but the

154

business men and commuters. 'It is essential that if Stratford is to remain on the railway map, we must have fast express trains serving the town,' said a statement last night. 'We consider that the 10 per cent increase in passengers on the Birmingham New Street–Euston electrified route is an indication of the vast untapped market for rail travel.'

The difficulty of getting to Stratford by rail is not all. The station itself, down beyond the cattle market, is some way from the centre of the town. The statement calls for feeder bus services between the bus station and the railway station.

(From the *Guardian*, 7.4.67)

Train services from Hunstanton
On Weekdays—
Trains depart for King's Lynn at: 7.0, 8.08, 10.22, 11.38, 13.35, 15.58, 16.58, 18.22, and 19.40. Sundays: 8.45, 12.50, 14.35, 17.40, 20.30 and 21.52.

There is no booking office and tickets must be obtained on the train. Through tickets to London, Cambridge, etc., are not available and must be obtained at King's Lynn. No porters are available and there are no Left Luggage facilities or parcels office. British Railways slogan: 'USE IT OR LOSE IT!'

(From *Spree*, 1965)

Schoolgirls who travel on the 8.20 a.m. train from Market Weighton via Pocklington and Stamford Bridge to York have written to Mr Tom Fraser, Minister of Transport, telling him he has been 'very inconsiderate' in giving his approval to withdrawal of passenger services on the York–Hull line.

The girls, who attend Mill Mount Grammar School, the Bar Convent and the York College for Girls, have not minced their words.

The correspondence between the girls and St Christopher House, headquarters of the Ministry of Transport in London, started after the school holidays and another letter on its way to Mr Fraser is telling him that 'We have no wish to stand in the cold and often in rain in Piccadilly, York, waiting for buses where there are no shelters'.

The Minister gave his approval for withdrawal of the services during the school holidays and 15 of the girls decided to sign a letter to the Minister asking him to change his mind.

155

They told him they would have to get up at 6.30 a.m. to catch the bus that will replace the train from Market Weighton.

A reply from the Ministry of Transport told the girls that Mr Fraser considered that improved services would meet the needs of people now using the railway, and pointed out that the Railways Board would provide additional trains on the York to Hull route via Selby.

Anne Buckland, aged 14, of Barmby Road, Pocklington said: 'That part of the letter is utter nonsense to us. It is obvious that nobody at the Ministry has looked at a map of Yorkshire or they would have seen that trains on the Hull to York via Selby line are no use to us at all.'

In their second letter to the Minister the girls have asked him: 'Have you looked at a map of East Yorkshire to see where Pocklington and Market Weighton are situated?'

(From *Yorkshire Evening Post* 7.10.65)

Shortly before the closure of British Rail's Keswick branch and while staying in Keswick, I went to get information about morning travel back to the West Riding as it then was. It seemed best to travel via Carlisle, but there was no convenient bus. But there was a train going to Carlisle. This, the only morning train suitable for returning holiday makers, left Keswick about 11 a.m., which was a bit late for folk going a good way. I asked confidently about connections at Carlisle for Leeds and Bradford. I was staggered to find that my train was timetabled to get me to Carlisle just four minutes *after* the departure of the Glasgow to London express via Leeds. And I was compelled to travel via Newcastle and down the East coast!

Sometime after this the Keswick branch was closed, and a trunk road is now blazing its way through the landscape in its place.

I have come across many examples of the mis-management of timetables—of what appears to be a deliberate way of sending passengers away empty-handed as part of a plot to cut down revenue and make a railway line useless, but never more so than in this case. And this in a National Park where cars do so much harm. If it wasn't a plot, it was sightless mis-management so appalling as to warrant a government investigation! How sad it is that these things have gone on, the cold slap in the customer's face, the wasting of fine viaducts and bridges and cuttings and tunnels fitting so well into the landscape. And then of course we have these horrible diesels which are always breaking down. Whereas the good old 'steamers' usually managed to make it home and us with them.

(From a letter)

Transport cuts blamed for deaths
(By our own Reporter)
Poor public transport services over the Christmas holiday may have been a direct cause of the increased road deaths, the National Council on Inland Transport has told Mrs Castle, Minister of Transport.

In a statement issued yesterday, the council said it considered that proposed integrated transport systems must meet the need of adequate services at holiday periods and on Sundays.

Mr Roger Calvert, its secretary, said: 'On British Railways generally there was a virtual shut down on Christmas Day.' He gave his home town, Watford, as an example of places where people were forced to go by road at Christmas. There were no train services on Christmas Day or Boxing Day, although it is on a main line to London, 18 miles away. No buses ran on Christmas Day, but London Transport put on a 'skeleton' service on Boxing Day.

Professor E. R. Hondelink, a transport consultant to the United Nations, said at his home at Amersham, Buckinghamshire, that the reduction of public transport services in France over the holiday was not a tenth of that carried out in Britain. In Holland there were full services on Christmas Day.

(From the *Guardian*, 30.12.66)

The cost of accidents
Sir,—In terms of human misery, no measurement is possible of the cost of a road accident death but, in terms of finance, a new viewpoint should be taken of the cost to a nation. On a national and international basis, this cost should be compared with very limited sums spent on road safety education. All nations should consider the cost from the more realistic

viewpoint of national income instead of from the mere administrative cost viewpoint.

In 1974 Britain had 6,900 deaths on the roads, with a further 82,100 people seriously injured, which is an appalling toll.

Under a national income 'cost' concept, assuming an average income for each fatal casualty of £3,000, this puts the loss to the nation, in national income, at £20 millions plus for one year only. Using 1974 as a base year, over an average working life of say only 20 years, allowing for casualties at both ends of the working life age span, the basic loss of national income to Britain, would total £400 millions. These are base year figures only, and from 1975, a further year's figures must be added to the cost; and this addition must be made on an annual basis.

Each road death costs approximately £20,000 in associated administrative and other costs, or, in total, some £138 millions each year. If the cost of some 82,000 serious road accidents were assessed in a similar way, the result in terms of cost to the nation is beyond levels envisaged by traditional Government thinking.

This staggering cost is unrecognized by our Government and internationally. Equally unrecognized, as contributing towards a solution, is the need for a statutory enforced, continuous programme of road safety education, thoughout all levels of our educational system.

At the present time road safety education in schools is non-statutory, very limited, and not sustained. Television campaigns are equally weak in impact. Within the total deaths on the road annual survey, certain aspects which should result in immediate Government action are deliberately under-publicized.

For example, at an international level, there are double casualty figures for male infants when compared with female infants of the same age group. In Britain we do not divide our infant road casualties by sex, but from my research into this aspect, statistics published for IQ testing and reading ability show an average 'IQ-maturity gap' which I title 'the male infant immaturity syndrome'. This can place an infant boy six months behind a female child in measured intelligence.

As a consequence, parents let their infant male children travel to school and on other local journeys, at the same age as a previous female child began such journeys. Female orientated teaching, from birth to seven years produces this syndrome, but the establishment ignores this concept because of the cost of a publicity campaign and educational changes that would be necessary.

Considered from a national income viewpoint, the cost of road accidents when compared with road safety education, is not compatible, or acceptable; and Britain must lead the world in reducing this self-imposed human misery by organized international research, and a model system of road safety education.

GEORGE RAWCLIFFE
Senior Lecturer
Blackpool College of Technology
(From the *Guardian*)

Appendix B

Sample Political Notes for Chapter 5
The Transport Act 1947
The Union's 15 M.P.s strongly supported the inclusion in the Transport Bill of 1947, provisions for the public ownership of the railways, docks, canals and road haulage services of the country though the various executives of the British Transport Commission. They persuaded Mr Barnes, the Minister of Transport, to make it an obligation for the Commission to prepare schemes for the integration of road and rail passenger services. But there were two important respects in which the final Act could be criticized. Yielding to the pressure of vested interests, Mr Barnes, at the Committee stage, withdrew clauses 56–58 of the Bill which had provided that vehicles under 'C' licence should be limited to a sphere of operation 40 miles from their base. Thus in the Act as finally drafted, virtually unlimited scope was given to the expansion of this type of road haulage.

The success of Public Transport, 1948–52
In 1947, the last year before nationalization, the railways had to be subsidized from the taxpayers to the extent of nearly £60 million to make good their revenue deficiencies. Under the management of the British Transport Commission the publicly-owned transport services of the nation earned operating surpluses from 1948 to 1956 inclusive, whilst from 1951–3 inclusive, profits of nearly £9 million were earned after all expenses, including interest charges, had been met. Freight carried on the railways in 1951, at nearly 285 million tons, was an all-time record and was achieved with 1,000 fewer engines than were in service in 1948. An outstanding success was achieved by the Road Haulage Executive whose trunk road haulage services, according to the *Economist* (29 November, 1952), traders relied upon as 'efficient and economical'. In consequence, this Executive's revenue sur-

plus rose rapidly from £1.1 million in 1948 to £8.9 million in 1953.

The Transport Act 1953

Had this state of affairs been allowed to continue the public would have become fully convinced of the superiority of a publicly-owned integrated transport system. But it is not a prominent feature of Tory Party policy to permit adverisement for the success of any form of common ownership. Furthermore, the private road haulage interests viewed the increasing revenue surpluses of the Road Haulage Executive with a mixture of envy and alarm. In the summer of 1949 the *Commercial Motor* urged road hauliers to contribute to the Conservative Central Office funds.

The victory of the Tories in the General Election of 29 October 1951 provided the opportunity, which was eagerly seized, to dismember the structure of the British Transport Commission. Under the Transport Act of 1953 a Road Haulage Disposal Board disposed of the bulk of the Road Haulage Executive's vehicles to private bidders at bargain prices. The British Transport Commission was thus deprived of 'the branch which bore the most fruit'. The A.G.M. of the N.U.R. rightly described this action as an 'act of sabotage inspired by selfish sectional interests' which would 'affect adversely the whole structure of transport'.

Unfortunately, the truth of this verdict was only too clearly demonstrated in the ensuing ten years. Deprived of some of its essential and most profitable assets, the Transport Commission could neither continue with its plans for transport integration nor yet avoid increasingly heavy financial deficits. By 1953 (before the new policy was applied) the indebtedness of the Commission had been reduced to £27 million. By the end of 1961 it had soared to £697 million. . . .

Railway modernization and reorganization

. . . Within two months of taking office as Minister of Transport, Mr Marples confessed to the House of Commons that until he took on his new job he thought he knew the meaning of the term 'vested interest'. Administrative decisions to switch to private firms orders for locomotives, rolling stock and component parts which could have been carried out more economically in railway workshops, and the provisions of Section 13 of the Transport Act, 1962, which forbid manufacture of 'road railers' in railway workshops, indicate that successive Conservative Governments have yielded to the pressure of these vested interests.

In January and February 1963 when deep snowdrifts made hundreds of roads impassable, many towns and villages relied solely on the railways for essential communications. When buses and delivery vans failed to reach Ashbourne in Derbyshire, a passenger service which had been closed for eight years was temporarily reopened by British Railways.

(From N.U.R. *Golden Jubilee Souvenir* 1963)

Select Bibliography

Education

Spock, Benjamin, *Bringing up Children in a Difficult Time,* Bodley Head, 1974

Whitehead, A. N., *The Aims of Education and Other Essays,* Ernest Benn, 1962

Neill, A. S., *Summerhill,* Pelican, 1968

Walmsley, J., and others, *Neill and Summerhill, A Man and his Work,* Penguin Education, 1969

Education and Religion

Keeling, M., *What is Right?,* S.C.M. Press, 1969

Robinson, J., *Honest to God,* S.C.M. Press, 1965

Taylor, J. V., *Enough is Enough,* S.C.M. Press, 1975

Furlong, M., *With Love to the Church,* Hodder, 1965

Buber, M., *I and Thou,* T. & T. Clark, Edinburgh, 1970

Morris, C., *Unyoung, Uncoloured, Unpoor,* Epworth Press, 1969

Education and the Social Scene

Perman, D., *Cublington, A Blueprint for Resistance,* Bodley Head, 1973

Ward, C., *Vandalism,* Architectural Press, 1973

Hutchings, M., and Caver, M., *Man's Dominion,* Hart-Davies, 1970

Davies, B., *Savage Luxury,* Souvenir Press, 1970

Harrison, R., *Animal Machines,* Vincent Stuart, 1964

Yarrow, A., *So Now You Know About Smoking,* British Medical Association (Family Doctor Booklet)

Report From Iron Mountain on the Possibility and Desirability of Peace, Penguin, 1968

People in Protest, York 2000, York, 1973

Leech, G. N., *English in Advertising,* Longmans, 1965

Packard, V., *The Waste Makers,* Penguin, 1965

Packard, V., *The Hidden Persuaders,* Longmans, 1957

Brown, J. A. C., *Techniques of Persuasion*, Penguin, 1961
Barr, J., *The Assaults on our Senses*, Sphere, 1970
Barr, J., *The Environmental Handbook: Action Guide for the U.K.*, Pan Books, 1971
Mabey, R., *The Pollution Handbook*, Penguin, 1975

Social Protest and Literature
Blake, William, Poetry and prose, *passim*
Forster, E. M., *Howard's End*
Henri, A., McGough, R., Patten, B., *The Mersey Sound* Penguin Modern Poets, No. 10, Penguin, 1974
Lawrence, D. H., Poems, essays, short stories
Shelley, P. B., *A Defence of Poetry*